CATHOLIC STA

THE GOSPEL OF
MATTHEW

With Meditation Prompts

Augustine Institute
Greenwood Village, CO

Nihil Obstat:
Father Michael Rapp, S.S.L.
Censor Librorum

Imprimatur:
+Most Reverend Samuel J. Aquila, S.T.L.
Archbishop of Denver
Denver, Colorado, USA
October 28, 2022

Graphic Design: Jeanné Reed

30 29 28 27 26 24 23 22   1 2 3 4 5 6 7

ISBN: 978-1-955305-70-9
Library of Congress Control Number: 2022949228

Printed in Canada

ABOUT THE
CATHOLIC STANDARD VERSION

This edition of the *Gospel according to Matthew* is the first installment of the Augustine Institute's new translation of Sacred Scripture, which will be called the *Catholic Standard Version* (CSV). "Catholic" because it will contain the full Catholic canon of 73 books, translated by a team of Catholic biblical scholars and theologians, according to the principles set forth by the living Magisterium of the Catholic Church. "Standard" because our aspiration is to set a new standard for Bibles in English by relying upon the most up-to-date findings in textual, linguistic, historical, and archaeological research, maintaining the highest level of accuracy in rendering the original languages, while also striving for an English expression that is marked by clarity and dignity. "Version" to signal that the CSV, as a vernacular translation of the written Word of God, can never rival the authority of the original texts of Scripture. As the work of translation progresses, the Institute plans to publish elegant editions of the four Gospels, the Psalms, and other important portions of Scripture for prayerful reading, serious study, catechesis, and evangelization by Catholics and other Christians throughout the English-speaking world.

TABLE OF
CONTENTS

THE GOSPEL ACCORDING TO MATTHEW..1

HOW TO PRAY WITH SCRIPTURE..105

MEDITATION PROMPTS..111

THE GOSPEL ACCORDING TO

MATTHEW[a]

The Genealogy of Jesus Christ

1 The book of the genealogy of Jesus Christ, the son of David, the son of Abraham.

[2] Abraham begot Isaac, Isaac begot Jacob, Jacob begot Judah and his brothers, [3] Judah begot Perez and Zerah by Tamar, Perez begot Hezron, Hezron begot Aram, [4] Aram begot Aminadab, Aminadab begot Nahshon, Nahshon begot Salmon, [5] Salmon begot Boaz by Rahab, Boaz begot Obed by Ruth, Obed begot Jesse, [6] and Jesse begot David the king.

David begot Solomon by the wife of Uriah, [7] Solomon begot Rehoboam, Rehoboam begot Abijah, Abijah begot Asa,[b] [8] Asa begot Jehoshaphat, Jehoshaphat begot Joram, Joram begot Uzziah, [9] Uzziah begot Jotham, Jotham begot Ahaz, Ahaz begot Hezekiah, [10] Hezekiah begot Manasseh, Manasseh begot Amon,[c] Amon begot Josiah, [11] and Josiah begot Jechoniah and his brothers, at the time of the Babylonian exile.

[12] After the Babylonian exile, Jechoniah begot Shealtiel, Shealtiel begot Zerubbabel, [13] Zerubbabel begot

---

[a] Some ancient manuscripts have *According to Matthew* [b] Some ancient manuscripts have *Asaph* [c] Some ancient manuscripts have *Amos*

Abiud, Abiud begot Eliakim, Eliakim begot Azor, [14] Azor begot Zadok, Zadok begot Achim, Achim begot Eliud, [15] Eliud begot Eleazar, Eleazar begot Matthan, Matthan begot Jacob, [16] and Jacob begot Joseph the husband of Mary, of whom Jesus was born, who is called the Christ.

[17] So all the generations from Abraham to David were fourteen generations; and from David to the Babylonian exile, fourteen generations; and from the Babylonian exile to the Christ, fourteen generations.

The Birth of Jesus Christ

[18] Now the birth of Jesus Christ took place in this way. When his mother Mary had been betrothed[a] to Joseph, before they came together, she was found to be with child of the Holy Spirit. [19] And Joseph her husband, being a righteous man and unwilling to expose her to shame, decided to divorce her secretly. [20] But while he was considering these things, behold, an angel of the Lord appeared to him in a dream, saying, "Joseph, son of David, do not fear to take Mary your wife, for the child conceived in her is of the Holy Spirit. [21] She will bear a son, and you shall call his name Jesus, for he will save his people from their sins." [22] Now all this took place so that what was spoken by the Lord through the prophet might be fulfilled,

---

[a] Legally married, but not yet living together as husband and wife

> [23] "Behold, the virgin shall be with
> child and bear a son, and they shall
> call his name Emmanuel,"[a]

which means, "God with us." [24] When Joseph rose from sleep, he did as the angel of the Lord commanded him and took his wife. [25] And he did not know[b] her until[c] she bore a son, and he called his name Jesus.

The Magi from the East

2 Now after Jesus was born in Bethlehem of Judea in the days of Herod the king, behold, magi from the east came to Jerusalem, [2] saying, "Where is he who was born king of the Jews? For we have seen his star at its rising and have come to worship him." [3] But when Herod the king heard this, he was troubled, and all Jerusalem with him. [4] And assembling all the chief priests and scribes of the people, he inquired of them where the Christ would be born. [5] They said to him, "In Bethlehem of Judea, for so it is written through the prophet,

> [6] 'And you Bethlehem, land of Judah, are
> by no means least among the rulers of
> Judah, for from you shall come a ruler,
> who will shepherd my people Israel.'"[d]

[7] Then Herod secretly called the magi and determined from them the time when the star appeared. [8] And he sent

---

[a] Isa 7:14 [b] To *know* is a biblical expression for marital relations; see Gen 4:1 [c] The word *until* (Greek *heos*) does not imply marital relations after Jesus' birth; compare Matt 28:20 [d] Mic 5:1; 2 Sam 5:2

them to Bethlehem and said, “Go and search diligently for the child. And when you have found him, report back to me, so that I too may come and worship him.”

[9] When they had heard the king, they departed. And behold, the star which they had seen at its rising went before them, until it came to rest over where the child was. [10] When they saw the star, they rejoiced with exceedingly great joy. [11] And coming into the house, they saw the child with Mary his mother, and they fell down and worshiped him. And opening their treasures, they presented him with gifts of gold, frankincense, and myrrh. [12] And having been warned in a dream not to return to Herod, they departed to their own country by another way.

The Flight to Egypt

[13] When they had departed, behold, an angel of the Lord appeared to Joseph in a dream, saying, “Rise, take the child and his mother and flee into Egypt, and stay there until I tell you, for Herod is about to search for the child, to destroy him.” [14] So he rose and took the child and his mother by night and went away into Egypt. [15] And he stayed there until the death of Herod, so that what was spoken by the Lord through the prophet might be fulfilled, “Out of Egypt I have called my son.”[d]

---

[d] Hos 11:1

The Massacre of the Infants

[16] Then, when Herod saw that he had been tricked by the magi, he was very angry. And he sent and killed all the children in Bethlehem and in all its surrounding regions, from two years old and under, according to the time he had ascertained from the magi. [17] Then was fulfilled what was spoken through Jeremiah the prophet,

> [18] "A voice was heard in Ramah,
> wailing and great lamentation,
> Rachel weeping for her children,
> and she would not be comforted,
> because they are no more."[a]

The Return from Egypt

[19] When Herod died, behold, an angel of the Lord appeared in a dream to Joseph in Egypt, [20] saying, "Rise, take the child and his mother and go to the land of Israel, for those who sought the life of the child are dead." [21] And he rose and took the child and his mother and came to the land of Israel. [22] But when he heard that Archelaus reigned over Judea in place of his father Herod, he was afraid to go there. And being warned in a dream, he went away to the territory of Galilee. [23] And he came and dwelt in a city called Nazareth, so that what was spoken through the prophets might be fulfilled, "He shall be called a Nazarene."[b]

---

[a] Jer 31:15 [b] Isa 11:1; Jer 23:5; 33:15; Zech 3:8; 6:12

The Preaching of John the Baptist

3 In those days John the Baptist came preaching in the wilderness of Judea, [2] saying, "Repent, for the kingdom of heaven is at hand!" [3] For this is he who was spoken of through Isaiah the prophet,

"A voice of one crying out
in the wilderness:
'Prepare the way of the Lord,
make his paths straight!' "[a]

[4] Now John himself wore a garment of camel's hair and a leather belt around his waist, and his food was locusts and wild honey. [5] Then Jerusalem and all Judea and all the region surrounding the Jordan went out to him, [6] and they were baptized by him in the Jordan river, confessing their sins.

[7] But when he saw many of the Pharisees and Sadducees coming for his baptism, he said to them, "You brood of vipers! Who warned you to flee from the coming wrath? [8] Bear fruit that is worthy of repentance. [9] Do not think to say to yourselves, 'We have Abraham as our father.' For I say to you, God is able to raise up children for Abraham from these stones! [10] Even now the axe is laid to the root of the trees. Therefore, every tree that does not bear good fruit is cut down and thrown into the fire. [11] I baptize you in water for repentance, but the one who

---

[a] Isa 40:3

is coming after me is mightier than I, whose sandals I am not worthy to carry. He will baptize you in the Holy Spirit and in fire. [12] His winnowing fork is in his hand, and he will cleanse his threshing floor and gather his wheat into the granary. But the chaff he will burn with unquenchable fire."

The Baptism of Jesus

[13] Then Jesus came from Galilee to John at the Jordan, to be baptized by him. [14] But John would have prevented him, saying, "I need to be baptized by you; yet you come to me?" [15] But Jesus answered and said to him, "Let it be so now, for in this way it is fitting for us to fulfill all righteousness." Then he consented. [16] And when Jesus was baptized, he immediately came up from the water, and behold, the heavens were opened to him,[a] and he saw the Spirit of God descending like a dove and coming upon him. [17] And behold, a voice from the heavens said, "This is my beloved Son, in whom I am well pleased."

The Temptations of Jesus

4 Then Jesus was led by the Spirit into the wilderness to be tempted by the devil. [2] And after fasting forty days and forty nights, he was hungry. [3] And the tempter came and said to him, "If you are the Son of God, command these stones to become loaves of bread." [4] But

---

[a] Some ancient manuscripts lack *to him*

he answered and said, "It is written,

'Man[a] shall not live by bread alone,
but by every word that comes
forth from the mouth of God.'"[b]

[5] Then the devil took him to the holy city and placed him on the ledge of the temple. [6] And he said to him, "If you are the Son of God, throw yourself down, for it is written,

'He will command his angels concerning you,
and on their hands they will bear you up,
lest you strike your foot against a stone.'"[c]

[7] Jesus said to him, "Again, it is written,

'You shall not put the Lord your God to
the test.'"[d]

[8] Again, the devil took him to a very high mountain and showed him all the kingdoms of the world and their glory. [9] And he said to him, "All these things I will give to you, if you will fall down and worship me." [10] Then Jesus said to him, "Be gone, Satan! For it is written,

'You shall worship the Lord your God,
and him only shall you serve.'"[e]

[11] Then the devil left him. And behold, angels came and ministered to him.

Jesus Begins to Preach in Galilee

[12] Now when he heard that John had been handed

---

[a] The collective singular *man* is inclusive of both men and women; see Gen 1:26–27; 5:2 [b] Deut 8:3 [c] Ps 91:11–12 [d] Deut 6:16 [e] Deut 6:13

over to the authorities, he went away into Galilee. [13] And leaving Nazareth, he came and dwelt in Capernaum by the sea, in the regions of Zebulun and Naphtali, [14] so that what was spoken through Isaiah the prophet might be fulfilled,

> [15] "Land of Zebulun and land of Naphtali,
> the way of the sea, beyond the Jordan,
> Galilee of the Gentiles.
> [16] The people who sit in darkness
> have seen a great light,
> and on those who sit in the
> region and shadow of death,
> light has dawned."[a]

[17] From then on, Jesus began to preach and to say, "Repent, for the kingdom of heaven is at hand!" [18] Now as he was walking beside the sea of Galilee, he saw two brothers: Simon, who is called Peter, and Andrew his brother. They were casting a net into the sea, for they were fishermen. [19] And he said to them, "Follow me, and I will make you fishers of men.[b]" [20] Immediately they left their nets and followed him.

[21] And going on from there, he saw two other brothers: James the son of Zebedee and John his brother. They were in the boat with Zebedee their father, mending their nets. And he called them. [22] Immediately they left the boat and their father and followed him.

---

[a] Isa 8:23–9:1 [b] Greek *anthropoi*, here includes both men and women

[23] And he went throughout all Galilee, teaching in their synagogues, preaching the gospel of the kingdom, and healing every disease and every sickness among the people. [24] So his fame spread throughout all Syria. And they brought to him all the sick who had various illnesses and were afflicted with torments, those possessed by demons, those who suffered from seizures, and paralytics, and he healed them. [25] And many crowds followed him from Galilee, the Decapolis, Jerusalem, Judea, and from beyond the Jordan.

The Beatitudes

5 When he saw the crowds, he went up the mountain. And when he sat down, his disciples came to him. [2] And he opened his mouth and taught them, saying:

[3] "Blessed[a] are the poor in spirit, for theirs is the kingdom of heaven.

[4] "Blessed are those who mourn, for they shall be comforted.

[5] "Blessed are the meek, for they shall inherit the earth.

[6] "Blessed are those who hunger and thirst for righteousness, for they shall be filled.

[7] "Blessed are the merciful, for they shall receive mercy.

---

[a] Or *Happy*. The same Greek word occurs at the beginning of each beatitude

[8] "Blessed are the pure in heart, for they shall see God.
[9] "Blessed are the peacemakers, for they shall be called sons of God.
[10] "Blessed are those who are persecuted for the sake of righteousness, for theirs is the kingdom of heaven.

[11] "Blessed are you whenever they insult you and persecute you and say all kinds of evil things against you falsely[a] because of me. [12] Rejoice and be glad, for your reward is great in heaven. For in the same way they persecuted the prophets who came before you.

Salt of the Earth, Light of the World

[13] "You are the salt of the earth. But if salt has lost its flavor, how will it be made salty again? It is no longer good for anything except to be thrown out and trampled underfoot.

[14] "You are the light of the world. A city set on a hill cannot be hidden. [15] Nor does anyone light a lamp and put it under a bushel basket, but on a lampstand, and it gives light to all in the house. [16] In the same way, let your light shine before others, so that they may see your good works and glorify your Father in heaven.

To Fulfill the Law and the Prophets

[17] "Do not think that I have come to abolish the law or the prophets. I have not come to abolish, but to fulfill.

---

[a] Some ancient manuscripts lack *falsely*

18 For amen, I say to you, until heaven and earth pass away, not one letter or part of a letter shall pass away from the law until all is accomplished. 19 Whoever therefore loosens one of the least of these commandments and teaches others to do so will be called least in the kingdom of heaven. But whoever does them and teaches them will be called great in the kingdom of heaven. 20 For I say to you, unless your righteousness surpasses that of the scribes and Pharisees, you will never enter the kingdom of heaven.

Murder and Anger

21 "You have heard that it was said to those of old, 'You shall not murder,' and 'Whoever murders will be liable to judgment.'[a] 22 But I say to you, everyone who is angry with his brother will be liable to judgment. And whoever says '*Raka*!'[b] to his brother will be liable to the Sanhedrin. And whoever says 'You fool!' will be liable to the Gehenna[c] of fire. 23 So if you bring your gift to the altar and there remember that your brother has anything against you, 24 leave your gift there before the altar and go. First be reconciled with your brother, and then come and offer your gift. 25 Make friends with your adversary quickly while you are with him on the way, lest your adversary hand you over to the judge, and the judge to the guard,

[a] Exod 20:13; Deut 5:17 [b] Aramaic insult, meaning something like *empty-head* [c] Aramaic for *valley of Hinnom*, a name for the realm of punishment after death; see Jer 19:1-6

and you be thrown into prison. [26] Amen, I say to you, you will never get out until you have paid the last penny.[a]

Adultery and Covetous Looks

[27] "You have heard that it was said, 'You shall not commit adultery.'[b] [28] But I say to you, everyone who looks at a woman in order to covet her has already committed adultery with her in his heart. [29] If your right eye leads you to sin, pluck it out and throw it away. It is better for you that one of your members perish than that your whole body be cast into Gehenna. [30] And if your right hand leads you to sin, cut it off and throw it away. It is better for you that one of your members perish than that your whole body go into Gehenna.

Divorce and Remarriage

[31] "It was said, 'Whoever divorces his wife must give her a bill of divorce.'[c] [32] But I say to you, whoever divorces his wife, except for a case of unlawful sexual relations,[d] makes her commit adultery.

Oaths and Swearing

[33] "Again, you have heard that it was said to those of old, 'You shall not swear falsely, but you shall keep your oaths to the Lord.'[a] [34] But I say to you, do not swear at all, either by heaven, because it is God's throne, [35] or by the

---

[a] A copper *quadrans*, the smallest of Roman coins [b] Exod 20:14; Deut 5:18 [c] Deut 24:1–4 [d] Greek *porneia*, can refer to a variety of unlawful sexual relations forbidden by Scripture, such as adultery by either husband or wife (Sir 23:16–23), incestuous unions (1 Cor 5:1), and prostitution (1 Cor 6:15-18)

earth, because it is his footstool, or by Jerusalem, because it is the city of the great King.[b] [36] Nor shall you swear by your head, because you cannot make one hair white or black. [37] Let your 'Yes' be 'Yes' and your 'No' be 'No.' Anything more than this is from the evil one.

Turn the Other Cheek

[38] "You have heard that it was said, 'An eye for an eye and a tooth for a tooth.'[c] [39] But I say to you, do not resist one who is evil. But if anyone strikes you on your right cheek, turn the other to him also. [40] And if anyone wants to sue you and take your tunic, give him your cloak as well. [41] And if anyone forces you to go one mile,[d] go with him two miles. [42] Give to the one who begs you, and do not turn away from the one who would borrow from you.

Hatred and Love of Enemies

[43] "You have heard that it was said, 'You shall love your neighbor and hate your enemy.'[e] [44] But I say to you, love your enemies and pray for those who persecute you, [45] so that you may be sons of your Father who is in heaven. For he makes his sun rise on the evil and the good, and he sends rain on the righteous and the unrighteous. [46] For if you love those who love you, what reward do you have? Do not even the tax collectors do the same? [47] And if you greet only your brothers, what more are you doing

---

[a] Num 30:2 [b] Ps 48:2 [c] Exod 21:24; Lev 24:20; Deut 19:21 [d] Greek *milion*, a walking distance of 1,000 paces [e] Lev 19:18; Deut 20:16–18; Ps 139:21–22

than others? Do not even the Gentiles do the same? [48] Be perfect, therefore, as your heavenly Father is perfect.

Almsgiving in Secret

6 "Beware of practicing your righteousness before others in order to be seen by them. Otherwise, you have no reward with your Father in heaven. [2] Therefore, when you give alms, do not blow a trumpet before you as the hypocrites do in the synagogues and in the streets, so that they may be praised by others. Amen, I say to you, they have their reward. [3] But when you give alms, do not let your left hand know what your right hand is doing, [4] so that your alms may be in secret. And your Father, who sees in secret, will repay you.

Prayer in Secret

[5] "When you pray, do not be like the hypocrites, for they love to stand and pray in the synagogues and on the street corners, so that they may be seen by others. Amen, I say to you, they have received their reward. [6] But you, when you pray, go into your inner room, and close your door and pray to your Father who is in secret. And your Father, who sees in secret, will repay you. [7] And when you pray, do not babble like the Gentiles, for they think they will be heard because of their many words. [8] Do not be like them, for your Father knows what you need before you ask him.

The Our Father

[9] "Pray, therefore, in this way:

'Our Father in heaven,
your name be hallowed,
[10] your kingdom come,
your will be done,
on earth as it is in heaven.
[11] Give us this day our daily[a] bread.
[12] And forgive us our debts,
as we forgive our debtors.
[13] And lead us not into temptation,[b]
but deliver us from the evil one.'[c] [d]

[14] For if you forgive others their trespasses, your heavenly Father will also forgive you. [15] But if you do not forgive them, neither will your Father forgive your trespasses.

Fasting in Secret

[16] "When you fast, do not look sad, like the hypocrites. For they change their appearance[e] so that their fasting may be seen by others. Amen, I say to you, they have their reward. [17] But when you fast, anoint your head and wash your face, [18] so that your fasting may not be seen by others, but by your Father who is in secret. And your Father, who sees in secret, will repay you.

---

[a] Greek *epiousios*, which can mean *essential, for today, for tomorrow, or supersubstantial* [b] Greek *peirasmos*, can mean *temptation* or *testing* [c] Or *evil* [d] Some later manuscripts include *For yours is the kingdom and the power and the glory forever. Amen.* [e] Either by not washing or by covering their heads; see Jer 14:3-4; Esth 6:12; 14:2

Treasure in Heaven

[19] "Do not store up for yourselves treasures on earth, where moth and rust consume, and where thieves break in and steal. [20] But store up for yourselves treasures in heaven, where moth and rust do not consume, and where thieves do not break in and steal. [21] For where your treasure is, there will your heart be also.

[22] "The lamp of the body is the eye. If, therefore, your eye is generous, your whole body will be full of light. [23] But if your eye is evil,[a] your whole body will be full of darkness. If, therefore, the light in you is darkness, how great is that darkness!

[24] "No one can serve two masters. For either he will hate the one and love the other, or he will be devoted to the one and despise the other. You cannot serve God and mammon.[b]

Do Not Be Anxious

[25] "Therefore, I say to you, do not be anxious about your life, what you will eat, or about your body, what you will wear. Is not life more than food and the body more than clothing? [26] Look at the birds of heaven. They neither sow, nor reap, nor gather into barns, and yet your heavenly Father feeds them. Are you not worth more than they? [27] Who among you by being anxious

---

[a] A person with an *evil eye* refuses to give to the poor and the needy; see Deut 15:9–10 [b] Aramaic for *wealth*

can add one cubit[a] to his span of life? [28] And why are you anxious about clothing? Consider the lilies of the field, how they grow. They neither toil nor spin, [29] yet I say to you, not even Solomon in all his glory was dressed like one of these. [30] But if God so clothes the grass of the field, which today is here and tomorrow is cast into the oven, will he not much more clothe you, O you of little faith? [31] Therefore, do not be anxious, saying, 'What will we eat?' or 'What will we drink?' or 'What will we wear?' [32] For the Gentiles seek after all these things, and your heavenly Father knows that you need them all. [33] But seek first the kingdom of God and his righteousness, and all these things will be added to you. [34] Therefore, do not be anxious about tomorrow, for tomorrow will be anxious for itself. Today's trouble is enough for today.

Do Not Judge

7 "Judge not, so that you may not be judged. [2] For with the judgment you make you will be judged, and the measure you give will be the measure you receive. [3] Why do you see the splinter in your brother's eye, but do not notice the wooden beam in your own eye? [4] Or how will you say to your brother, 'Let me remove the splinter from your eye,' when behold, there is a wooden beam in your own eye? [5] You hypocrite! First remove the

---

[a] About 18 inches or 45 centimeters

wooden beam from your own eye, and then you will see clearly to remove the splinter from your brother's eye.

Dogs and Swine

[6] "Do not give what is holy[a] to dogs, or cast your pearls before swine, lest they trample them underfoot and turn and tear you in pieces.

Ask, Seek, Knock

[7] "Ask, and it shall be given to you; seek, and you shall find; knock, and it shall be opened to you. [8] For everyone who asks receives, and the one who seeks finds, and to the one who knocks, it shall be opened. [9] Who among you, if his son asks him for bread, will give him a stone? [10] Or if he asks for a fish, will give him a snake? [11] So if you, who are evil, know how to give good gifts to your children, how much more will your Father in heaven give good things to those who ask him!

The Golden Rule

[12] "Therefore, do to others whatever you would have them do to you. For this is the law and the prophets.

The Two Ways

[13] "Enter through the narrow gate, for the gate is wide and the way is easy that leads to destruction, and those who enter through it are many. [14] But the gate is narrow

---

[a] Or *the holy food*; see Lev 22:14–16; Exod 22:31

and the way is hard that leads to life, and those who find it are few.

By Their Fruits You Shall Know Them

[15] "Beware of false prophets, who come to you in sheep's clothing but inwardly are ravenous wolves. [16] By their fruits you shall know them. Are grapes gathered from thorns, or figs from thistles? [17] In the same way, every good tree bears good fruit, but a bad tree bears evil fruit. [18] A good tree cannot bear evil fruit, nor can a bad tree bear good fruit. [19] Every tree not bearing good fruit is cut down and cast into the fire. [20] So by their fruits you shall know them.

[21] "Not everyone who says to me, 'Lord, Lord,' will enter the kingdom of heaven, but rather the one who does the will of my Father in heaven. [22] Many will say to me on that day, 'Lord, Lord, did we not prophesy in your name, and cast out demons in your name, and do many deeds of power in your name?' [23] Then I will declare to them, 'I never knew you. Depart from me, you evildoers.'"[a]

The Wise Man and the Foolish Man

[24] "Everyone therefore who hears these words of mine and does them will be like a wise man who built his house on the rock. [25] The rain fell, the floods came, and the winds blew and beat on that house. But it did not

---

[a] Literally *workers of lawlessness*; see Ps 6:9

fall, for it was founded on the rock. [26] And everyone who hears these words of mine and does not do them will be like a foolish man who built his house upon the sand. [27] The rain fell, the floods came, and the winds blew and beat upon that house. And it fell, and great was its fall."

[28] Now when Jesus had finished these words, the crowds were astonished at his teaching. [29] For he taught them as one having authority, and not as their scribes.

Jesus Heals a Leper

8 When he came down from the mountain, many crowds followed him. [2] And behold, a leper came and worshiped him, saying, "Lord, if you will it, you can make me clean." [3] And he stretched out his hand and touched him, saying, "I will it; be made clean." And immediately his leprosy[a] was cleansed. [4] And Jesus said to him, "See that you tell no one. But go, show yourself to the priest and offer the gift that Moses commanded, for a testimony to them."

The Faith of the Centurion

[5] And when he entered Capernaum, a centurion came to him and begged him, [6] saying, "Lord, my servant[b] lies at home paralyzed, suffering terribly." [7] And he said to him, "I will come and heal him." [8] The centurion answered and said, "Lord, I am not worthy that you should enter under

---

[a] Greek *lepra*, refers to a variety of skin diseases; see Lev 13 [b] Or *child*

my roof, but only say the word, and my servant shall be healed. [9] For I too am a man under authority, with soldiers under me. And I say to this one, 'Go,' and he goes; and to another, 'Come,' and he comes; and to my servant, 'Do this,' and he does it."

[10] When Jesus heard this, he marveled and said to those who followed him, "Amen, I say to you, with no one in Israel have I found such faith! [11] And I say to you, many shall come from east and west and recline at table with Abraham, Isaac, and Jacob, in the kingdom of heaven. [12] But the sons of the kingdom shall be cast out into the outer darkness, where there shall be weeping and gnashing of teeth." [13] And Jesus said to the centurion, "Go. As you have believed, so let it be done for you." And his servant was healed in that hour.

Jesus Heals the Sick

[14] When Jesus entered Peter's house, he saw his mother-in-law lying down and burning with a fever. [15] So he touched her hand, and the fever left her. And she rose up and ministered to him.

[16] When it was evening, they brought to him many who were demon-possessed. And he cast out the spirits with a word and healed all who were sick, [17] so that what was spoken through Isaiah the prophet might be fulfilled,

"He took our infirmities,
and bore our diseases."[a]

Following Jesus

[18] Now when Jesus saw a crowd around him, he gave orders to depart to the other side. [19] And a scribe came and said to him, "Teacher, I will follow you wherever you go." [20] And Jesus said to him, "Foxes have holes, and the birds of heaven have nests, but the Son of Man has nowhere to lay his head." [21] And another of his disciples said to him, "Lord, allow me first to go and bury my father." [22] But Jesus said to him, "Follow me, and let the dead bury their dead."

Jesus Stills a Storm

[23] And when he got into the boat, his disciples followed him. [24] And behold, a great storm arose on the sea, so that the boat was being swamped by the waves. But he was asleep. [25] And they came and woke him, saying, "Lord, save us, we are perishing!" [26] And he said to them, "Why are you fearful, O you of little faith?" Then he rose and rebuked the winds and the sea. And there was a great calm. [27] But the men marveled and said, "What kind of man is this, that even the winds and the sea obey him?"

---

[a] Isa 53:4

Jesus Heals Two Demon-Possessed Men

28 When he came to the other side, to the region of the Gadarenes,[a] two demon-possessed men met him, coming out of the tombs. They were so violent that no one was ever able to travel that way. 29 And behold, they cried out, saying, "What have you to do with us, Son of God? Have you come here to torment us before the time?" 30 Now a herd of many swine was feeding far from them. 31 So the demons begged him, saying, "If you cast us out, send us into the herd of swine." 32 And he said to them, "Go." When they came out, they went into the swine. And behold, the whole herd rushed down the bank into the sea and died in the waters. 33 And the herders fled, and they went away into the city and told everything, including what had happened to the demon-possessed men. 34 And behold, the whole city came out to meet Jesus. And when they saw him, they begged him to leave their region.

Jesus Heals a Paralytic

9 After getting into a boat, he crossed over to the other side and came into his own city. 2 And behold, they brought to him a paralytic lying on a mat. And when Jesus saw their faith, he said to the paralytic, "Take heart, son; your sins are forgiven." 3 And behold, some of

---

[a] Some ancient manuscripts have *Gerasenes* or *Gergesenes*

the scribes said to themselves, "This man is blaspheming!" [4] But when Jesus saw their thoughts, he said, "Why do you think evil in your hearts? [5] For which is easier? To say, 'Your sins are forgiven,' or to say, 'Rise and walk?' [6] But so that you may know that the Son of Man has authority on earth to forgive sins"—then he said to the paralytic, "Rise, take up your mat, and go to your house." [7] And he rose and departed to his house. [8] When the crowds saw it, they were afraid, and they glorified God, who had given such authority to men.

Jesus Calls Matthew the Tax Collector

[9] As Jesus was passing along from there, he saw a man named Matthew sitting at the tax booth, and he said to him, "Follow me." And he rose and followed him.

[10] And as he was reclining at table in the house, behold, many tax collectors and sinners came and were reclining with Jesus and his disciples. [11] And when the Pharisees saw it, they said to his disciples, "Why does your teacher eat with tax collectors and sinners?" [12] But when he heard it, he said, "Those who are healthy have no need for a physician, but those who are sick. [13] But go and learn what this means, 'I desire mercy, and not sacrifice.'[a] For I have come not to call the righteous, but sinners."

---

[a] Hos 6:6

A Question about Fasting

[14] Then the disciples of John came to him and said, "Why do we and the Pharisees fast frequently,[a] but your disciples do not fast?" [15] And Jesus said to them, "Can the groomsmen[b] mourn as long as the bridegroom is with them? But the days will come when the bridegroom will be taken away from them, and then they shall fast. [16] No one puts a piece of unshrunken cloth on an old garment, for the patch pulls away from the garment, and a worse tear is made. [17] Nor do they put new wine into old wineskins. Otherwise the skins burst, the wine spills out, and the skins are destroyed. But they put new wine into new wineskins, and both are preserved."

A Ruler's Daughter and the Woman with a Hemorrhage

[18] While he was saying these things to them, behold, a ruler came and worshiped him, saying, "My daughter has just died. But come, lay your hand upon her, and she will live." [19] And Jesus rose up and followed him, along with his disciples.

[20] And behold, a woman who had been suffering with a hemorrhage for twelve years came up behind him and touched the fringe[c] of his garment. [21] For she said to herself, "If only I touch his garment, I will be saved." [22] But when Jesus turned around and saw her, he said, "Take heart, daughter; your faith has saved you." And the woman was healed from that hour.

---

[a] Some ancient manuscripts lack *frequently* [b] Literally *the sons of the bridal chamber* [c] Tassels worn on the four corners of an outer garment as a reminder to keep the commandments; see Num 15:37–40; Deut 22:12

[23] And when Jesus came into the ruler's house and saw the flute-players and the crowd making a commotion, [24] he said, "Go away! For the girl is not dead, but sleeping." And they laughed at him. [25] But when the crowd was sent out, he went inside and took her hand, and the girl arose. [26] And the news of this went out into all that land.

Jesus Heals Two Blind Men

[27] When Jesus passed on from there, two blind men followed him, crying out and saying, "Have mercy on us, Son of David!" [28] And when he came into the house, the blind men came to him. And Jesus said to them, "Do you believe that I am able to do this?" They said to him, "Yes, Lord." [29] Then he touched their eyes, saying, "As you have believed, so let it be done to you." [30] And their eyes were opened. And Jesus sternly warned them, saying, "See that no one knows of it." [31] But they went out and spread word of him in all that land.

Jesus Heals a Mute Demon-Possessed Man

[32] As they were going out, behold, a demon-possessed man who was mute was brought to him. [33] And when the demon had been cast out, the mute man spoke, and the crowds marveled, saying, "Never has anything like this appeared in Israel!" [34] But the Pharisees said, "By the prince[a] of demons he casts out demons."

---

[a] Or *ruler*

The Harvest and the Laborers

[35] And Jesus went around all the cities and villages, teaching in their synagogues, preaching the gospel of the kingdom, and healing every disease and every sickness. [36] But when he saw the crowds, he had compassion on them, because they were weary and scattered like sheep without a shepherd. [37] Then he said to his disciples, "The harvest is plentiful, but the laborers are few. [38] Therefore, ask the Lord of the harvest to send out laborers into his harvest."

Jesus Calls the Twelve Disciples

10 After calling his twelve disciples to himself, he gave them authority over unclean spirits, to cast them out, and to heal every disease and every sickness. [2] Now these are the names of the twelve apostles: first, Simon, who is called Peter, and Andrew his brother; then James the son of Zebedee and John his brother; [3] Philip and Bartholomew; Thomas and Matthew the tax collector; James the son of Alphaeus and Thaddaeus; [4] Simon the Cananean[a] and Judas Iscariot, who betrayed him.

Jesus Sends the Twelve

[5] Jesus sent out these twelve and commanded them, saying, "Do not go along a road of the Gentiles, and do not enter any city of the Samaritans. [6] Go rather to the

---

[a] From the Aramaic *qani'an*, meaning *enthusiast* or *zealot*

lost sheep of the house of Israel. [7] And preach as you go, saying, 'The kingdom of heaven is at hand.' [8] Heal the sick, raise the dead, cleanse lepers, cast out demons. Freely you have received; freely give. [9] Acquire no gold, or silver, or copper to put in your belts; [10] and take no bag for the journey, or two cloaks, or sandals, or a staff. For the laborer deserves his food.

[11] "And whatever city or village you enter, search for who is worthy in it, and remain there until you go away. [12] When you enter a house, greet it. [13] And if the house is worthy, let your peace come upon it; but if it is not worthy, let your peace return to you. [14] And whoever will not receive you or hear your words, when you go out of that house or city, shake off the dust from your feet. [15] Amen, I say to you, it shall be more tolerable for the land of Sodom and Gomorrah on the day of judgment than for that city.

You Will Be Hated by All

[16] "Behold, I send you out as sheep in the midst of wolves. Therefore, be wise as serpents and innocent as doves. [17] But beware of men, for they will hand you over to sanhedrins[a] and flog you in their synagogues. [18] And you will be brought before governors and kings for my sake, for testimony to them and the Gentiles. [19] But when

---

[a] Jewish ruling councils located in several cities in the land of Israel

they hand you over, do not be anxious about how you are to speak or what you are to say, for what you are to say will be given to you in that hour. [20] For it is not you who speak, but the Spirit of your Father who speaks in you.

[21] "Brother will hand over brother to death, and a father his child, and children will rise up against parents and put them to death. [22] And you will be hated by all because of my name. But the one who endures to the end shall be saved. [23] Whenever they persecute you in one city, flee to another. For amen, I say to you, you will not finish going through the cities of Israel before the Son of Man comes.

[24] "A disciple is not above his teacher, nor a servant above his master. [25] It is enough for the disciple to be like his teacher, and the servant like his master. If they have called the master of the house Beelzebul,[a] how much more the members of his house!

Do Not Fear Them

[26] "So do not fear them. For nothing is hidden that will not be revealed, and nothing secret that will not be known. [27] What I say to you in the dark, say in the light, and what you hear whispered in your ear, preach upon the housetops. [28] And do not fear those who kill the body but are not able to kill the soul. Rather, fear him who is

---

[a] Aramaic for *lord of flies*

able to destroy both soul and body in Gehenna. [29] Are not two sparrows sold for a copper coin? Yet not one of them will fall to the ground apart from your Father. [30] Even the hairs of your head are all counted. [31] So do not fear. You are worth more than many sparrows.

[32] "Everyone therefore who confesses me before men, I also will confess before my Father who is in heaven. [33] But whoever denies me before men, I also will deny before my Father who is in heaven.

Not Peace, But a Sword

[34] "Do not think that I have come to cast peace upon the earth. I have not come to cast peace, but a sword. [35] For I have come to turn

> 'a man against his father,
> and a daughter against her mother,
> and a daughter-in-law against
> her mother-in-law.
> [36] And a man's enemies will be
> from his own household.'[a]

[37] "Whoever loves father or mother more than me is not worthy of me, and whoever loves son or daughter more than me is not worthy of me. [38] And whoever does not take up his cross and follow me is not worthy of me. [39] Whoever finds his life will lose it, and whoever loses his life for my sake will find it.

---

[a] Mic 7:6

The Reward for Receiving Disciples

[40] "Whoever receives you receives me, and whoever receives me receives him who sent me. [41] Whoever receives a prophet in the name of a prophet will receive a prophet's reward, and whoever receives a righteous person in the name of a righteous person will receive the reward of the righteous. [42] And whoever gives even a cup of cold water to drink to one of these little ones in the name of a disciple—amen, I say to you, he shall by no means lose his reward."

11 Now when Jesus had finished instructing his twelve disciples, he left there to teach and to preach in their cities.

Jesus and John the Baptist

[2] Now when John heard in prison about the works of the Christ, he sent word through his disciples [3] and said to him, "Are you the one who is to come, or shall we wait for another?" [4] And Jesus answered and said to them, "Go tell John what you hear and see: [5] the blind receive their sight, the lame walk, the lepers[a] are cleansed, the deaf hear, the dead are raised, and the poor have good news proclaimed to them.[b] [6] And blessed is he who is not scandalized by me." [7] As they were going, Jesus began to

---

[a] Greek *lepros*, refers to a person with a skin disease; see Lev 13
[b] Isa 26:19; 29:18; 35:5

say to the crowds regarding John, "What did you go out into the wilderness to see? A reed shaken by the wind? [8] What then did you go out to see? A man clothed in soft garments? Behold, those who wear soft garments are in the houses of kings. [9] What then did you go out to see? A prophet? Yes, I say to you, and more than a prophet. [10] This is he of whom it is written,

> 'Behold, I am sending my
> messenger before your face,
> who will prepare your way before you.'[a]

[11] Amen, I say to you, among those born of women there has arisen no one greater than John the Baptist. Yet the one who is least in the kingdom of heaven is greater than he.[12] And from the days of John the Baptist until now, the kingdom of heaven has suffered violence, and the violent seize it by force. [13] For all the prophets and the law prophesied until John, [14] and if you are willing to accept it, he is Elijah who is to come. [15] Whoever has ears, let him hear!

[16] "But to what shall I compare this generation? It is like children sitting in the marketplaces, who call out to others, [17] saying,

> 'We played the flute for you, but you did
> not dance,
> we sang a lament, but you did not mourn.'

[18] For John came neither eating nor drinking, and they

---

[a] Exod 23:20; Mal 3:1

say, 'He has a demon!' [19] The Son of Man came eating and drinking, and they say, 'Behold a glutton and a drunkard, a friend of tax-collectors and sinners!' But wisdom is justified by her works."

Jesus Reprimands Those Who Do Not Repent

[20] Then he began to reprimand the cities in which most of his deeds of power were done, because they did not repent. [21] "Woe to you, Chorazin! Woe to you, Bethsaida! For if the deeds of power done in you had been done in Tyre and Sidon, they would have repented long ago in sackcloth and ashes. [22] But I say to you, it shall be more tolerable for Tyre and Sidon on the day of judgment than for you. [23] And you, Capernaum, will you be exalted to heaven? You shall be brought down to hell.[a] For if the deeds of power done in you had been done in Sodom, it would have remained until this day. [24] But I say to you, it shall be more tolerable for the land of Sodom on the day of judgment than for you."

The Father and the Son

[25] At that time Jesus said, "I praise you, Father, Lord of heaven and earth, because you have hidden these things from the wise and understanding and have revealed them to little ones.[b] [26] Yes, Father, for so it has seemed good in your sight. [27] All things have been handed over to me by my

---

[a] Greek *Hades*, the realm of the dead [b] Or *the childlike*; literally, *infants*

Father. No one knows the Son except the Father, and no one knows the Father except the Son and anyone to whom the Son chooses to reveal him.

[28] "Come to me, all you who are weary and burdened, and I will give you rest. [29] Take my yoke upon you and learn from me, for I am meek and humble in heart, and you will find rest for your souls. [30] For my yoke is sweet, and my burden is light."

The Lord of the Sabbath

12 At that time, Jesus went through the grain fields on the Sabbath. Now his disciples were hungry, and they began to pick the heads of grain and eat them. [2] But when the Pharisees saw it, they said to him, "Behold, your disciples are doing what is not lawful on the Sabbath." [3] But he said to them, "Have you not read what David did, when he was hungry, and those with him? [4] How he went into the house of God and ate the bread of the Presence, which was not lawful for him to eat, nor for those with him, but only for the priests?[a] [5] Or have you not read in the law that on the Sabbath the priests in the temple profane the Sabbath, yet are innocent?[b] [6] But I say to you, something greater than the temple is here. [7] And if you had known what this means, 'I desire mercy, and not sacrifice,'[c] you would not have condemned the innocent. [8] For the Son of Man is Lord of the Sabbath."

---

[a] 1 Sam 21:1–6 [b] Num 28:1–10 [c] Hos 6:6

The Man with the Withered Hand

[9] When he left there, he entered their synagogue. [10] And behold, there was a man with a withered hand. And they asked him, saying, "Is it lawful to heal on the Sabbath?"—so that they might accuse him. [11] And he said to them, "Which one of you who has one sheep, if it falls into a pit on the Sabbath, will not take hold of it and lift it out? [12] How much more valuable is a person than a sheep! Therefore, it is lawful to do good on the Sabbath." [13] Then he said to the man, "Stretch out your hand." And he stretched it out, and it was restored to health like his other hand. [14] Then the Pharisees went out and took counsel against him, in order to destroy him.

The Chosen Servant

[15] But Jesus, knowing this, withdrew from there. And many crowds followed him, and he healed them all. [16] And he warned them not to make him known, [17] so that what was spoken through Isaiah the prophet might be fulfilled,

> [18] "Behold my servant,
> whom I have chosen,
> my beloved, in whom my
> soul is well pleased;
> I will put my Spirit upon him,
> and he will proclaim judgment
> to the Gentiles.

[19] He will not quarrel or shout,
nor will anyone hear his
voice in the streets.
[20] A bruised reed he will not break,
and a smoldering wick he
will not quench,
until he brings judgment to victory.
[21] And in his name the
Gentiles will hope."[a]

Jesus and Beelzebul

[22] Then a demon-possessed man who was blind and mute was brought to him. And he healed him, so that the mute man was able to speak and to see. [23] And all the crowds were amazed and said, "Can this be the son of David?" [24] But when the Pharisees heard it, they said, "It is only by Beelzebul,[b] the prince[c] of demons, that this man casts out demons." [25] But knowing their thoughts, he said to them, "Every kingdom divided against itself is made desolate, and every city or house divided against itself will not stand. [26] And if Satan casts out Satan, he is divided against himself. How then will his kingdom stand? [27] If I cast out demons by Beelzebul, by whom do your sons cast them out? Therefore they will be your judges. [28] But if by the Spirit of God I cast out demons, then the kingdom of

---

[a] Isa 42:1–4 [b] Aramaic for *lord of flies* [c] Or *ruler*

God has come upon you. [29] Or how can someone break into the house of a strong man and steal his things, unless he first binds the strong man? Then he will plunder his house. [30] Whoever is not with me is against me, and whoever does not gather with me scatters.

Blasphemy Against the Holy Spirit

[31] "Therefore I say to you, people will be forgiven for every sin and blasphemy, but blasphemy against the Spirit will not be forgiven. [32] Whoever speaks a word against the Son of Man will be forgiven, but whoever speaks against the Holy Spirit will not be forgiven, either in this age or in the age to come.

The Good Tree and the Bad Tree

[33] "Either make the tree good and its fruit good, or else make the tree bad and its fruit bad. For the tree is known by its fruit. [34] You brood of vipers! How can you speak good things when you are evil? For out of the abundance of the heart the mouth speaks. [35] The good person out of his good treasure brings forth good, and the evil person out of his evil treasure brings forth evil. [36] I say to you, on the day of judgment, you will give an account for every careless word you speak. [37] For by your words you will be justified, and by your words you will be condemned."

The Sign of Jonah

[38] Then some of the scribes and Pharisees answered him, saying, "Teacher, we wish to see a sign from you." [39] But he answered and said to them, "An evil and adulterous generation seeks after a sign, but no sign will be given to it except the sign of Jonah the prophet.[40] For just as Jonah was in the belly of the fish three days and three nights,[a] so will the Son of Man be in the heart of the earth three days and three nights. [41] The men of Nineveh will arise at the judgment with this generation and condemn it, for they repented at the preaching of Jonah. And behold, something greater than Jonah is here! [42] The queen of the south will be raised up at the judgment with this generation and condemn it, for she came from the ends of the earth to hear the wisdom of Solomon. And behold, something greater than Solomon is here!

The Unclean Spirit

[43] "Whenever an unclean spirit has gone out of a person, it goes about through waterless places seeking rest, but it finds none. [44] Then it says, 'I will return to my house from which I came.' And when it comes, it finds it empty, swept, and put in order. [45] Then it goes and takes with it seven other spirits more evil than itself,

---

[a] Jonah 1:17

and they enter and dwell there. And the last state of that person is worse than the first. So will it be with this evil generation."

The Mother and Brothers of Jesus

[46] While he was still speaking to the crowds, behold, his mother and his brothers[a] stood outside, seeking to speak with him. [47] Then someone said to him, "Behold, your mother and your brothers are standing outside, seeking to speak with you."[b] [48] But he answered and said to the one speaking to him, "Who is my mother, and who are my brothers?" [49] And he stretched out his hand over his disciples, and said, "Behold, my mother and my brothers. [50] For whoever does the will of my Father who is in heaven is my brother, and sister, and mother."

Jesus Teaches the Crowd on the Shore

13 On that day, Jesus went out of the house and sat beside the sea. [2] And many crowds were gathered to him, so that he got into a boat and sat down. And all the crowd stood on the shore.

The Parable of the Sower

[3] And he spoke many things to them in parables, saying, "Behold, the sower went out to sow. [4] And while he sowed, some seeds fell beside the path, and the birds

---

[a] Greek *adelphos*, can refer to a blood-brother or male relative; see 1 Chron 23:21-22 (LXX) [b] Some ancient manuscripts lack verse 47

came and ate them up. [5] Others fell upon rocky ground where they did not have much soil, and immediately they sprang up, because they had no depth of soil. [6] But when the sun came up they were scorched, and because they had no root, they withered. [7] Others fell among thorns, and the thorns grew up and choked them. [8] But others fell on good soil, and produced fruit: some a hundredfold, some sixty, some thirty. [9] Whoever has ears, let him hear!"

Why Jesus Speaks in Parables

[10] And the disciples came and said to him, "Why do you speak to them in parables?" [11] He answered and said to them, "To you it has been given to know the mysteries of the kingdom of heaven, but to them it has not been given. [12] For whoever has, more will be given to him, and he will have in abundance. But whoever does not have, even what he has will be taken away from him. [13] For this reason I speak to them in parables: because seeing, they do not see, and hearing, they do not hear, nor do they understand. [14] In them is fulfilled the prophecy of Isaiah, which says,

'Hearing, you will hear,
but not understand,
and seeing, you will see, but not perceive.
[15] For the heart of this
people has grown fat,

and their ears have grown
hard of hearing;
and they have closed their eyes,
lest they see with their eyes,
and hear with their ears,
and understand with their heart,
and they turn, and I heal them.'[a]

[16] But blessed are your eyes, for they see, and your ears, for they hear. [17] Amen, I say to you, many prophets and righteous people longed to see what you see, and did not see it, and to hear what you hear, and did not hear it!

The Parable of the Sower Explained

[18] "Hear then the parable of the sower: [19] when anyone hears the word of the kingdom and does not understand, the evil one comes and takes away what was sown in his heart—this is what was sown beside the path. [20] As for what was sown upon the rocky ground—this is the one who hears the word, and immediately receives it with joy. [21] Yet he has no root in himself, but lasts only for a little while. And when tribulation or persecution happens because of the word, immediately he falls away. [22] As for what was sown among the thorns—this is the one who hears the word, but the cares of this age and the deception of riches choke the word, and it becomes fruitless. [23] As

---

[a] Isa 6:9–10

for what was sown upon good soil—this is the one who hears the word and understands it. He indeed bears fruit and produces: in one case a hundredfold, in another sixty, and in another thirty."

The Weeds and the Wheat

[24] He put another parable before them, saying, "The kingdom of heaven may be compared to a man who sowed good seed in his field. [25] But while everyone slept, his enemy came and sowed weeds in the midst of the wheat, and went away. [26] When the plants sprouted and bore grain, the weeds also appeared. [27] Then the servants of the master of the house came and said to him, 'Master, did you not sow good seed in your field? Where then did the weeds come from?' [28] He said to them, 'An enemy has done this.' The servants said to him, 'Then do you want us to go and gather them up?' [29] But he said, 'No, lest in gathering up the weeds, you uproot the wheat along with them. [30] Let both grow together until the harvest. And at the time of the harvest, I will say to the reapers, First gather the weeds and bind them in bundles to burn them, but gather the wheat into my granary.'"

The Mustard Seed

[31] He put another parable before them, saying, "The kingdom of heaven is like a mustard seed, which a man

took and sowed in his field. [32] It is the smallest of all seeds, but when it is grown, it is the greatest of herbs and becomes a tree, so that the birds of heaven come and nest in its branches."

The Leaven

[33] He spoke to them another parable, "The kingdom of heaven is like leaven, which a woman took and hid in three measures of flour until it was all leavened."

The Parables and the Prophet

[34] All these things Jesus spoke in parables to the crowds. He spoke nothing to them without a parable, [35] so that what was spoken through the prophet might be fulfilled,

"I will open my mouth in parables;
I will proclaim things hidden since
the foundation of the world."[a]

The Parable of the Weeds Explained

[36] Then he dismissed the crowds and went into the house. And his disciples came to him, saying, "Explain to us the parable of the weeds of the field." [37] He answered and said, "The one who sows the good seed is the Son of Man; [38] the field is the world, and the good seed are the sons of the kingdom. But the weeds are the sons of the evil one; [39] the enemy who sowed them is the devil; the harvest

---

[a] Ps 78:2

is the end of the age, and the reapers are the angels. [40] Just as the weeds are gathered and burned with fire, so will it be at the end of the age. [41] The Son of Man will send forth his angels, and they will gather out of his kingdom all who lead others to sin and those who commit lawlessness. [42] And they will cast them into the furnace of fire, where there shall be weeping and gnashing of teeth. [43] Then the righteous will shine like the sun in the kingdom of their Father. Whoever has ears, let him hear!

The Hidden Treasure

[44] "The kingdom of heaven is like a treasure hidden in a field, which a man found and hid. Then, in his joy, he went and sold all that he had and bought that field.

The Pearl of Great Price

[45] "Again, the kingdom of heaven is like a merchant seeking fine pearls. [46] When he found one pearl of great price, he went and sold all that he had and bought it.

The Dragnet

[47] "Again, the kingdom of heaven is like a dragnet that was cast into the sea and gathered fish of every kind. [48] When it was full, they pulled it up on the shore and sat down and gathered the good into vessels, but the bad they cast out. [49] So will it be at the end of the age. The

angels will come forth and separate the evil from the midst of the righteous, [50] and they will cast them into the furnace of fire, where there shall be weeping and gnashing of teeth.

The Scribe in the Kingdom of Heaven

[51] "Have you understood all these things?" They said to him, "Yes." [52] He said to them, "For this reason, every scribe who has become a disciple of the kingdom of heaven is like the master of a house, who brings out of his treasure both the new and the old."

A Prophet in His Hometown

[53] Now when Jesus had finished these parables, he went away from there. [54] And when he came into his hometown, he taught them in their synagogue, so that they were astonished and said, "Where did this man get this wisdom and these powers? [55] Is this not the carpenter's son? Is not his mother called Mary, and are not his brothers[a] James and Joseph and Simon and Jude?[b] [56] And his sisters,[c] are they not all with us? So where did this man get all this?" [57] And they were scandalized by him. But Jesus said to them, "No prophet is without honor except in his hometown and in his own house." [58] And he did not do many deeds of power there, because of their unbelief.

---

[a] Greek *adelphos*, can refer to a blood-brother or male relative; see 1 Chron 23:21-22 (LXX) [b] Greek *Ioudas*, which can also be rendered as *Judah* or *Judas* [c] Greek *adelphe*, can refer to a blood-sister or female relative; see Tob 7:9; 8:4, 7

The Beheading of John the Baptist

14 At that time Herod the tetrarch[a] heard of the fame of Jesus, [2] and he said to his servants, "This is John the Baptist! He has been raised from the dead, and this is why these powers are at work in him." [3] For Herod had arrested John, bound him, and put him in prison because of Herodias, the wife of Philip his brother. [4] For John had said to him, "It is not lawful for you to have her." [5] And though he wanted to put him to death, he was afraid of the crowd, because they held him to be a prophet.

[6] But when Herod's birthday came, the daughter of Herodias danced in their midst and pleased Herod. [7] So he promised with an oath to give her whatever she asked. [8] And prompted by her mother, she said, "Give me here on a platter the head of John the Baptist." [9] Although the king was grieved, for the sake of the oath and those who sat at table with him, he ordered it to be given. [10] And he sent and beheaded John in prison. [11] And his head was brought in on a platter and given to the girl, and she brought it to her mother. [12] Then his disciples came and took the body and buried it. And they went and told Jesus.

The Feeding of the Five Thousand

[13] Now when Jesus heard of this, he withdrew from there in a boat to a deserted place by himself. But when

---

[a] A low-level prince subject to Roman authorities

the crowds heard, they followed him on foot from the cities. [14] When he came ashore, he saw the great crowd, and he had compassion on them and healed their sick. [15] And when it was evening, the disciples came to him and said, "This is a deserted place, and the hour is now past. Send the crowd away, so that they may go into the villages and buy food for themselves." [16] But Jesus said to them, "They need not go away. You give them something to eat." [17] They said to him, "We have nothing here except five loaves of bread and two fish." [18] So he said, "Bring them here to me." [19] And he ordered the crowd to recline on the grass. Taking the five loaves and the two fish and looking up to heaven, he said the blessing, broke the loaves, and gave them to his disciples. And his disciples gave them to the crowd. [20] Then they all ate and were filled. And they took up what remained of the broken pieces, twelve baskets[a] full. [21] Those who had eaten were about five thousand men, besides women and children.

Jesus Walks on the Sea

[22] And immediately he made his disciples get into the boat and go before him to the other side, while he sent away the crowds. [23] And when he had sent the crowds away, he went up the mountain by himself to pray. And when it was evening, he was there alone. [24] Now the boat was already miles[b] away from the land, being battered

---

[a] Greek *kophinos*, a straw-lined basket used by Jews for carrying food while traveling [b] Literally *many stadia*. A single Greek *stadion* is about 607 feet or 185 meters

by the waves, for the wind was against it. [25] And in the fourth watch of the night,[a] he came to them, walking on the sea. [26] And when the disciples saw him walking on the sea, they were frightened, saying, "It is a ghost!" And they cried out in fear. [27] But immediately Jesus spoke to them, saying, "Take heart! I am;[b] do not fear." [28] And Peter answered him and said, "Lord, if it is you, command me to come to you on the waters." [29] And he said, "Come!" And when Peter stepped out of the boat, he walked on the waters and came to Jesus. [30] But when he saw the strong wind, he was afraid. And beginning to sink, he cried out, saying, "Lord, save me!" [31] And immediately Jesus stretched out his hand, took hold of him, and said to him, "O you of little faith, why did you doubt?" [32] And when they climbed into the boat, the wind ceased. [33] Then those who were in the boat worshiped him, saying, "Truly you are the Son of God!"

Jesus in the Land of Gennesaret

[34] And when they had crossed over, they came ashore to Gennesaret. [35] And when the people of that place recognized him, they sent word into all that surrounding region and brought to him all the sick. [36] And they were begging him that they might touch only the fringe[c] of his garment. And all who touched it were healed.

---

[a] Between 3am and 6am [b] Or *I am he*; see Exod 3:14; Isa 43:10 [c] Tassels worn on the four corners of an outer garment as a reminder to keep the commandments; see Num 15:37-40; Deut 22:12

The Pharisees and Their Tradition

15 Then Pharisees and scribes came to Jesus from Jerusalem, saying, [2] "Why do your disciples transgress the tradition of the elders? For they do not wash their hands when they eat." [3] But he answered and said to them, "Why do you transgress the commandment of God for the sake of your tradition? [4] For God said, 'Honor your father and mother,'[a] and, 'Whoever curses his father or mother must die.'[b] [5] But you say, 'Whoever says to his father or mother, "Whatever you are owed from me is a gift to God," [6] he need not honor his father.' You have made void the word of God for the sake of your tradition. [7] You hypocrites! Well did Isaiah prophesy about you, saying,

> [8] 'This people honors me with their lips,
> but their heart is far away from me.
> [9] In vain do they worship me,
> teaching as doctrines the
> commandments of men.'"[c]

What Defiles a Person

[10] And he called the crowd to himself and said to them, "Hear and understand: [11] it is not what goes into the mouth that defiles a person, but what comes out of the mouth; this defiles a person." [12] Then his disciples

---

[a] Exod 20:12; Deut 5:16 [b] Exod 21:17; Lev 20:9 [c] Isa 29:13

came and said to him, "Do you know that the Pharisees were scandalized when they heard this saying?" [13] But he answered and said, "Every plant that my heavenly Father has not planted will be uprooted. [14] Leave them alone. They are blind guides of the blind. If one blind person leads another, both will fall into a pit." [15] Then Peter answered and said to him, "Explain to us this parable." [16] And Jesus said, "Are you also still without understanding? [17] Do you not perceive that everything that goes into the mouth enters the stomach and is expelled into the sewer? [18] But those things which proceed from the mouth come out of the heart, and they defile a person. [19] For out of the heart come evil thoughts, murders, adulteries, sexual sins,[a] thefts, false testimonies, blasphemies. [20] These are the things that defile a person, but to eat with unwashed hands does not defile a person."

The Canaanite Woman

[21] Then Jesus went away from there and departed into the district of Tyre and Sidon. [22] And behold, a Canaanite woman from that region came and cried out, saying, "Have mercy on me, Lord, Son of David! My daughter is cruelly tormented by a demon." [23] But he did not answer her a word. And his disciples came and begged him, saying, "Send her away, for she is crying out after us." [24] But he

---

[a] Greek *porneiai* (plural), refers to a range of illicit actions, such as fornication, prostitution, and homosexual acts; see Tob 4:12; Wis 14:12, 24–27

answered and said, "I was sent only to the lost sheep of the house of Israel." [25] Then she came and worshiped him, saying, "Lord, help me!" [26] But he answered and said, "It is not good to take the bread of the children and throw it to the dogs." [27] But she said, "Yes, Lord, but even the dogs eat the crumbs that fall from their masters' table." [28] Then Jesus answered and said to her, "O woman, great is your faith! Let it be done for you as you wish." And her daughter was healed from that hour.

Jesus Heals the Crowds on the Mountain

[29] And Jesus left there and walked along beside the sea of Galilee. And he went up the mountain, where he sat down. [30] Many crowds came to him, bringing with them those who were lame, blind, maimed, mute, and many others, and they laid them down at his feet. And he healed them, [31] so that the crowd marveled when they saw the mute speaking, the maimed made whole, the lame walking, and the blind seeing. And they glorified the God of Israel.

The Feeding of the Four Thousand

[32] Then Jesus called his disciples to himself and said, "I have compassion for the crowd, since they have remained with me for three days now and have nothing to eat. And I am not willing to send them away fasting, lest they faint on the road." [33] His disciples said to him, "Where can we

get enough bread in this desolate place to satisfy such a crowd?" 34 And Jesus said to them, "How many loaves do you have?" And they said, "Seven, and a few small fish." 35 Then he ordered the crowd to sit on the ground. 36 And he took the seven loaves and the fish, and having given thanks, he broke them and gave them to his disciples, and the disciples gave them to the crowds. 37 Then they all ate and were filled. And they took up what remained of the broken pieces, seven baskets[a] full. 38 Those who had eaten were four thousand men, besides women and children. 39 And after he sent away the crowds, he got into the boat and came into the region of Magadan.[b]

The Signs of the Times

16 Now the Pharisees and Sadducees came to test him, and they asked him to show them a sign from heaven. 2 He answered and said to them, "When it is evening, you say, 'It will be good weather, for the sky is red.' 3 And in the morning, 'It will be bad weather today, for the sky is red and threatening.' You know how to judge the face of the sky, but not the signs of the times.[c] 4 An evil and adulterous generation seeks a sign, but no sign will be given to it except the sign of Jonah." And he left them and went away.

---

[a] Greek *spuris*, a basket used by Gentiles for carrying food [b] Some ancient manuscripts have *Magdala* [c] Some ancient manuscripts lack part of verse 2 and all of verse 3 ("*When it is evening... of the times.*")

The Leaven of the Pharisees and the Sadducees

[5] And when his disciples came to the other side, they had forgotten to bring bread. [6] Then Jesus said to them, "Watch, and beware of the leaven of the Pharisees and the Sadducees." [7] And they were discussing it among themselves, saying, "We did not bring bread!" [8] But knowing this, Jesus said, "O you of little faith, why are you discussing among yourselves that you have no bread? [9] Do you not yet understand? Or do you not remember the five loaves for the five thousand, and how many baskets you took up? [10] Or the seven loaves for the four thousand, and how many baskets you took up? [11] How do you not understand that I did not speak to you about bread? Beware of the leaven of the Pharisees and the Sadducees." [12] Then they realized that he had not told them to beware of the leaven of bread, but of the teaching of the Pharisees and the Sadducees.

Jesus, Peter, and the Keys of the Kingdom

[13] When Jesus came into the district of Caesarea Philippi, he asked his disciples, "Who do people say that the Son of Man is?" [14] And they said, "Some say John the Baptist, others Elijah, still others say Jeremiah or one of the prophets." [15] He said to them, "But you, who do you say that I am?" [16] Simon Peter answered and said, "You are the Christ, the Son of the living God." [17] And Jesus answered

and said to him, "Blessed are you, Simon Bar-Jonah,[a] for flesh and blood has not revealed this to you, but my Father who is in heaven. [18] And I say to you, you are Peter, and upon this rock[b] I will build my Church, and the gates of hell[c] shall not prevail against it. [19] I will give you the keys of the kingdom of heaven. Whatever you bind on earth shall be bound in heaven, and whatever you loose on earth shall be loosed in heaven." [20] Then he commanded his disciples to tell no one that he was the Christ.

Peter Rebukes Jesus

[21] From then on Jesus began to show his disciples that he must go to Jerusalem and suffer many things from the elders and chief priests and scribes, and be killed, and on the third day be raised. [22] Then Peter took him aside and began to rebuke him, saying, "Far be it from you, Lord! Surely this shall never happen to you." [23] But he turned and said to Peter, "Get behind me, Satan! You are a stumbling block to me, for you are not thinking the things of God, but the things of men."

Whoever Loses His Life Will Find It

[24] Then Jesus said to his disciples, "If anyone wants to come after me, let him deny himself and take up his cross and follow me. [25] For whoever would save his life[d] will lose it, but whoever loses his life for my sake will

---

[a] Aramaic for *son of Jonah* [b] Greek *petra* ("rock") is a play on the Greek *petros* ("Peter"), Jesus' name for Simon [c] Greek *Hades*, the realm of the dead [d] Greek *psychē*, meaning *life* or *soul*

find it. [26] For what shall it profit someone if he gains the whole world, but suffers the loss of his soul?[a] Or what will someone give in exchange for his soul? [27] For the Son of Man is about to come in the glory of his Father with his angels, and then he will repay each person according to his works.[b] [28] Amen, I say to you, there are some standing here who shall not taste death until they see the Son of Man coming in his kingdom."

The Transfiguration

17 After six days, Jesus took with him Peter and James and John his brother and led them up a high mountain by themselves. [2] And he was transfigured before them, and his face shone like the sun, and his garments became white as light. [3] And behold, Moses and Elijah appeared to them and were talking with him. [4] Then Peter answered and said to Jesus, "Lord, it is good for us to be here. If you wish, I will make three tabernacles here, one for you, one for Moses, and one for Elijah." [5] While he was still speaking, behold, a luminous cloud overshadowed them. And behold, a voice from the cloud said, "This is my beloved Son, in whom I am well pleased. Listen to him!" [6] And when the disciples heard this, they fell on their faces and were filled with fear. [7] But Jesus came and touched them and said, "Rise, and do not fear." [8] And when they

---

[a] Greek *psychē*, meaning *life* or *soul* [b] Ps 63:12

lifted up their eyes, they saw no one but Jesus alone. [9] And as they were coming down from the mountain, Jesus commanded them saying, "Tell no one about the vision until the Son of Man is raised from the dead."

Elijah Has Already Come

[10] And his disciples asked him, "Why then do the scribes say that Elijah must come first?" [11] He answered and said, "Elijah does come, and he will restore all things. [12] But I say to you that Elijah has already come, and they did not recognize him, but they did to him whatever they wanted. So too the Son of Man is about to suffer at their hands." [13] Then the disciples understood that he had spoken to them of John the Baptist.

Jesus Casts Out a Demon from a Man's Son

[14] And when they came to the crowd, a man came and knelt before him, [15] saying, "Lord, have mercy on my son, for he has seizures and suffers terribly. For he often falls into the fire, and often into the water. [16] So I brought him to your disciples, but they were not able to heal him." [17] Then Jesus answered and said, "O faithless and perverse generation, how long will I be with you? How long will I endure you? Bring him here to me." [18] And Jesus rebuked the demon, and it came out of him, and the child was healed from that hour. [19] Then the disciples came to Jesus privately and said, "Why were we

not able to cast it out?" [20] And he said to them, "Because of your little faith. For amen, I say to you, if you have faith like a mustard seed, you will say to this mountain, 'Move from here to there,' and it will move. And nothing will be impossible for you."[a]

Jesus Predicts His Death and Resurrection

[22] And while they were gathering in Galilee, Jesus said to them, "The Son of Man is about to be betrayed into the hands of men. [23] They will kill him, and on the third day he will be raised." And they were very sorrowful.

Jesus, Peter, and the Temple Tax

[24] When they came into Capernaum, the collectors of the temple tax[b] came to Peter and said: "Does your teacher not pay the temple tax? [25] He said, "Yes." And when he came into the house, Jesus spoke to him first, asking, "What do you think, Simon? From whom do the kings of the earth collect toll or tax? From their sons, or from others?" [26] Peter said to him, "From others." Jesus said to him, "Then the sons are free. [27] Yet, lest we scandalize them, go to the sea, cast a fishhook, and take the first fish that comes up. And when you open its mouth, you will find a silver coin worth four drachmas.[c] Take that, and give it to them for me and for you."

---

[a] Some ancient manuscripts include as verse 21: *But this kind does not come out except by prayer and fasting* [b] Greek *didrachmon*, a coin required of Jewish men as an annual payment to the Jerusalem temple [c] Greek *stater*, a coin worth two *didrachma* and thus equal to an annual temple payment for two Jewish men

The Greatest in the Kingdom

18 At that hour, the disciples came to Jesus, saying, "Who then is greatest in the kingdom of heaven?" [2] And calling a little child to himself, he stood him in their midst [3] and said, "Amen, I say to you, unless you turn and become like little children, you will never enter the kingdom of heaven. [4] Therefore, whoever humbles himself like this little child is the greatest in the kingdom of heaven. [5] And whoever receives one such little child in my name, receives me.

Scandals

[6] "But whoever leads one of these little ones who believe in me into sin, it would be better for him to have a great millstone[a] hung around his neck and be drowned in the depths of the sea. [7] Woe to the world because of scandals! For scandals must come, but woe to the one through whom the scandal comes!

[8] "So if your hand or your foot leads you to sin, cut it off and throw it away. It is better for you to enter life maimed or lame than to have two hands or two feet and be cast into the eternal fire. [9] And if your eye leads you to sin, pluck it out and throw it away. It is better for you to enter life with one eye than to have two eyes and be cast into the Gehenna of fire.

---

[a] Literally *donkey's millstone*; not a small stone used for a hand mill, but one so heavy that it was turned by a donkey

Angels in Heaven

[10] "See that you do not despise one of these little ones. For I say to you, in heaven their angels continually see the face of my Father who is in heaven.[a]

The Lost Sheep

[12] "What do you think? If a man has a hundred sheep, and one of them goes astray, will he not leave the ninety-nine on the mountains and go in search of the one gone astray? [13] Amen, I say to you, if he finds it, he rejoices over it more than over the ninety-nine that did not go astray. [14] In the same way, it is not the will of your Father who is in heaven that one of these little ones should perish.

If Your Brother Sins Against You

[15] "If your brother sins against you, go, tell him his fault between you and him alone. If he listens to you, you have gained your brother. [16] But if he does not listen, take with you one or two others, so that 'every word may be established from the mouth of two or three witnesses.'[b] [17] And if he refuses to listen to them, tell the church. But if he refuses to listen even to the church, let him be to you like a Gentile or a tax collector. [18] Amen, I say to you, whatever you bind on earth shall be bound in heaven, and whatever you loose on earth shall be loosed in heaven. [19] Again, amen I say to you, if two of you agree

---

[a] Some ancient manuscripts include as verse 11: *For the Son of Man came to save the lost.* [b] Deut 19:15

on earth about anything they ask, it shall be done for them by my Father who is in heaven. [20] For where two or three are gathered in my name, there I am in the midst of them."

The Unforgiving Servant

[21] Then Peter came and said to him, "Lord, how many times will my brother sin against me and I forgive him? Up to seven times?" [22] Jesus said to him, "I say to you, not up to seven times, but up to seventy-seven times.[a]

[23] "For this reason, the kingdom of heaven may be compared to a king who wished to settle accounts with his servants. [24] When he began to settle accounts, one was brought to him who owed ten thousand talents.[b] [25] But because he did not have the money to pay, his master ordered him to be sold, along with his wife and children and all that he had, and payment to be made. [26] So the servant fell down and worshiped him, saying, 'Have patience with me, and I will pay you everything'. [27] Then the lord of that servant, moved with compassion, released him and forgave him the debt. [28] But when the same servant went out, he found one of his fellow servants who owed him one hundred denarii.[c] And he seized him and began choking him, saying, 'Pay what you owe!' [29] So his fellow servant fell down and begged

---

[a] Or *seventy times seven times*; see Gen 4:24 [b] Greek *talanton*; a single talent was worth about 6,000 days' wages for a laborer [c] Roman silver coins; a single *denarius* was a common daily wage for a laborer

him, saying, 'Have patience with me, and I will pay you.' [30] But he would not. Instead he went and cast him into prison, until he should pay what was owed.

[31] "For this reason, when his fellow servants saw what had taken place, they were extremely sorrowful. So they went and told their lord all that had taken place. [32] Then his lord called him and said to him, 'You evil servant! I forgave you all that debt because you begged me. [33] Should you not have had mercy on your fellow servant, just as I had mercy on you?' [34] And the lord was angry, and he handed him over to the torturers until he should pay all the debt. [35] So my heavenly Father will also do to each one of you, if you do not forgive your brother from your heart."

Jesus Comes into Judea

19 Now when Jesus had finished these words, he departed from Galilee and came into the regions of Judea beyond the Jordan. [2] And many crowds followed him, and he healed them there.

Divorce and Remarriage

[3] And Pharisees came to him in order to test him, saying, "Is it lawful for a man to divorce his wife for any reason?" [4] And he answered and said, "Have you not read that from the beginning, the Creator 'made them

male and female'[a] [5] and said, 'For this reason a man shall leave his father and mother and be joined to his wife, and the two shall become one flesh'?[b] [6] So they are no longer two, but one flesh. Therefore, what God has yoked together, let no one separate." [7] They said to him, "Why then did Moses command us to give her a bill of divorce and send her away?"[c] [8] He said to them, "Moses permitted you to divorce your wives because of your hardness of heart, but from the beginning it was not so. [9] But I say to you, whoever divorces his wife, except on the basis of unlawful sexual relations,[d] and marries another, commits adultery."[e]

Eunuchs for the Sake of the Kingdom

[10] The disciples said to him, "If this is the case of a man with his wife, it is better not to marry!" [11] But he said to them, "Not everyone receives this word, but only those to whom it is given. [12] For there are some eunuchs who were born eunuchs from their mother's womb, and there are some who were made eunuchs by men, and there are some who have made themselves eunuchs for the sake of the kingdom of heaven. Whoever is able to receive this, let him receive it."

Let the Little Children Come to Me

[13] Then little children were brought to him so that

---

[a] Gen 1:27 [b] Gen 2:24 [c] Deut 24:1–4 [d] Greek *porneia*, can refer to a variety of unlawful sexual relations forbidden by Scripture, such as adultery by either husband or wife (Sir 23:16–23), incestuous unions (1 Cor 5:1), and prostitution (1 Cor 6:15-18) [e] Some ancient manuscripts include *And whoever marries a divorced woman commits adultery.*

he might lay hands on them and pray. And the disciples rebuked them. [14] But Jesus said, "Let the little children come to me, and do not prevent them, for the kingdom of heaven belongs to such as these." [15] And he laid his hands on them and went away from there.

The Rich Young Man

[16] And behold, someone came to him and said, "Teacher, what good must I do to have eternal life?" [17] But he said to him, "Why do you ask me about the good? There is one who is good. If you wish to enter into life, keep the commandments."

[18] He said to him, "Which ones?" Jesus said, "'You shall not murder, You shall not commit adultery, You shall not steal, You shall not bear false witness,[a] [19] Honor your father and mother,[b] and You shall love your neighbor as yourself.'"[c] [20] The young man said to him, "All these I have kept. What do I still lack?" [21] Jesus said to him, "If you wish to be perfect, go, sell what you have and give to the poor, and you will have treasure in heaven. And come, follow me." [22] But when the young man heard this word, he went away grieving, for he had many possessions.

The Rich and the Kingdom of Heaven

[23] Then Jesus said to his disciples, "Amen, I say to

---

[a] Exod 20:13–16; Deut 5:17–20 [b] Exod 20:12; Deut 5:16 [c] Lev 19:18

you, it will be difficult for one who is rich to enter the kingdom of heaven. [24] Again I say to you, it is easier for a camel to go through the eye of a needle than for a rich man to enter the kingdom of God." [25] When the disciples heard it, they were utterly astonished and said, "Who then can be saved?" [26] But Jesus looked at them and said, "With man, this is impossible, but with God, all things are possible."

The Twelve Thrones and the Twelve Tribes

[27] Then Peter answered and said to him, "See, we have left everything and followed you. What then will we have?" [28] And Jesus said to him, "Amen, I say to you, in the new creation, when the Son of Man sits upon his throne of glory, you who have followed me will also sit upon twelve thrones, judging the twelve tribes of Israel. [29] And everyone who has left houses, or brothers, or sisters, or father, or mother, or children, or fields for the sake of my name, will receive a hundredfold and inherit eternal life. [30] But many who are first shall be last, and the last first.

The Workers in the Vineyard

20 "For the kingdom of heaven is like the master of a house who went out early in the morning to hire workers for his vineyard. [2] When he had agreed to give the workers a denarius[a] for the day, he sent them

---

[a] A Roman silver coin, a common daily wage for a laborer

into his vineyard. [3] And going out at about the third hour,[a] he saw others standing idle in the marketplace. [4] And he said to them, 'You also go into the vineyard, and whatever is just, I will give you.' [5] So they went. And going out again around the sixth hour[b] and the ninth hour,[c] he did likewise. [6] Around the eleventh hour,[d] he went out and found others standing and said to them, 'Why do you stand here idle the whole day?' [7] They said to him, 'Because no one hired us.' He said to them, 'You also go into the vineyard.'

[8] "When it was evening, the master of the vineyard said to his foreman, 'Call the workers and pay them their wage, beginning with the last and proceeding to the first.' [9] And those who came around the eleventh hour each received one denarius. [10] And when the first came, they thought they would receive more, but they also received one denarius. [11] And when they received it, they murmured against the master of the house, [12] saying, 'These last worked one hour, and you have made them equal to us, who endured the burden of the day and the burning heat!' [13] But he answered one of them and said, 'Friend, I did you no injustice. Did you not agree with me for a denarius? [14] Take what is yours and go, for I wish to give this last one exactly what I gave you. [15] Or am I not allowed to do what I will with what is mine? Or is your

---

[a] About 9am [b] About noon [c] About 3pm [d] About 5pm

eye evil[a] because I am good?' [16] In this way, the last shall be first and the first shall be last."

Jesus Predicts His Death and Resurrection a Third Time

[17] As Jesus was going up to Jerusalem, he took the twelve disciples aside by themselves, and he said to them on the way, [18] "Behold, we are going up to Jerusalem, and the Son of Man will be handed over to the chief priests and scribes, and they will condemn him to death. [19] And they will hand him over to the Gentiles to be mocked and scourged and crucified, and on the third day he will be raised."

The Request of the Mother of James and John

[20] Then the mother of the sons of Zebedee came to him with her sons. And worshiping him, she asked him for something. [21] But he said to her, "What do you wish?" She said to him, "Declare that these two sons of mine may sit, one at your right hand and one at your left, in your kingdom." [22] But Jesus answered and said, "You do not know what you are asking. Are you able to drink the cup that I am about to drink?" They said to him, "We are able." [23] He said to them, "You will drink my cup, but to sit at my right hand and at my left is not mine to give, but is for those for whom it is prepared by my Father."

[24] And when the ten heard it, they were indignant at the two brothers. [25] But Jesus called them to himself and

---

[a] A person with an *evil eye* is greedy; see Prov 28:22

said, "You know that the rulers of the Gentiles lord it over them, and their great ones exercise authority over them. [26] It shall not be so among you. But whoever wishes to become great among you must be your minister,[a] [27] and whoever wishes to be first among you must be your servant, [28] just as the Son of Man did not come to be served but to serve, and to give his life as a ransom for many."

Jesus Heals Two Blind Men

[29] As they were going out from Jericho, a great crowd followed him. [30] And behold, two blind men were sitting beside the road. When they heard that Jesus was passing by, they cried out, saying, "Have mercy on us, Lord, son of David!" [31] And the crowd rebuked them in order to silence them. But they cried out louder and said, "Have mercy on us, Lord, son of David!" [32] And Jesus stood still, and he called them and said, "What do you want me to do for you?" [33] They said to him, "Lord, let our eyes be opened." [34] So Jesus had compassion on them and touched their eyes, and immediately they were able to see, and they followed him.

Jesus Enters into Jerusalem

21 When they drew near to Jerusalem and came to Bethphage on the Mount of Olives, Jesus then sent two disciples, [2] saying to them, "Go into the village opposite you, and immediately you will find a donkey

---

[a] Greek *diakonos*

tied and a colt with her. Untie them and bring them to me. [3] And if anyone says anything to you, say, 'The Lord has need of them,' and he will send them immediately."[a] [4] Now this took place so that what was spoken through the prophet might be fulfilled,

[5] "Tell the daughter of Zion,
'Behold, your King comes to you,
meek and riding on a donkey,
and on a colt, the foal of
a beast of burden.'"[b]

[6] And the disciples went and did as Jesus commanded them. [7] They brought the donkey and the colt and placed their garments on them, and he sat on them. [8] And a very large crowd spread their garments on the road. Others cut branches from the trees and spread them on the road. [9] And the crowds that went before him and those that followed cried out, saying,

"Hosanna[c] to the Son of David!
'Blessed is he who comes in
the name of the Lord!'
Hosanna in the highest!"[d]

[10] And when he entered Jerusalem, the whole city shook, saying, "Who is this?" [11] The crowds were saying, "This is the prophet Jesus from Nazareth of Galilee." [12] And Jesus went into the temple and cast out all those who sold

---

[a] Or *'The Lord has need of them, but he will send them back immediately.'*
[b] Isa 62:11; Zech 9:9 [c] Aramaic for *Save us* or *Help us* [d] Ps 118:25–26

and bought in the temple. And he overturned the tables of the moneychangers and the seats of those who sold doves. [13] And he said to them, "It is written,

'My house shall be called
a house of prayer,'
but you are making it 'a den of thieves.'"[a]

[14] And the blind and the lame came to him in the temple, and he healed them. [15] When the chief priests and the scribes saw the wonders he had done and the children crying out in the temple, saying, "Hosanna to the Son of David!" they were indignant. [16] And they said to him, "Do you hear what these people are saying?" Jesus said to them, "Yes. Have you never read:

'Out of the mouths of
babes[b] and nurslings,
you have perfected praise'?"[c]

[17] And leaving them, he went out of the city to Bethany and spent the night there.

Jesus and the Fig Tree

[18] Now in the morning, as he was returning to the city, he was hungry. [19] Seeing a fig tree on the way, he went to it but found nothing on it except leaves. And he said to it, "May no fruit ever come from you again!" And the fig tree withered at once. [20] When the disciples saw it,

---

[a] Or *robbers*; see Isa 56:7; Jer 7:11 [b] Or *infants* [c] Ps 8:3

they marveled and said, "How did the fig tree wither at once?" [21] Jesus answered and said to them, "Amen, I say to you, if you have faith and do not doubt, not only will you do what was done to the fig tree, but even if you say to this mountain, 'Be lifted up and cast into the sea,' it will be done. [22] And whatever you ask in prayer, you will receive, if you have faith."

The Authority of Jesus and John the Baptist

[23] When he had come into the temple, the chief priests and the elders of the people came to him as he was teaching and said, "By what authority do you do these things? And who gave you this authority?" [24] And Jesus answered and said to them, "I too will ask you one question, and if you answer me, then I will also tell you by what authority I do these things. [25] The baptism of John: where was it from? From heaven, or from men?" And they discussed it among themselves saying, "If we say, 'From heaven,' he will say to us, 'Why then did you not believe him?' [26] But if we say, 'From men,' we fear the crowd, for they all hold John to be a prophet." [27] So they answered Jesus and said, "We do not know." And he said to them, "Neither will I tell you by what authority I do these things."

The Two Children

[28] "What do you think? A man had two children. And

he came to the first and said, 'Child, go and work in the vineyard today.' 29 He answered and said, 'I will not.' But later he changed his mind and went. 30 And he came to the other and said likewise. And he answered and said, 'I will, sir.'[d] But he did not go. 31 Which of the two did the will of the father?" They said, "The first." Jesus said to them, "Amen, I say to you, tax collectors and prostitutes are entering the kingdom of God ahead of you, 32 for John came to you in the way of righteousness, and you did not believe him. But tax collectors and prostitutes believed him. Yet when you saw it, even then you did not change your mind and believe him.

The Wicked Tenants

33 "Hear another parable: there was a master of a house who planted a vineyard, put a fence around it, dug a winepress in it, and built a tower. Then he rented it out to tenant farmers and went on a journey. 34 And when the season for fruit drew near, he sent his servants to the tenants to collect its fruits. 35 And the tenants took his servants, beat one, killed another, and stoned another. 36 Again, he sent other servants, more than the first, and they did the same to them. 37 Afterward he sent his son to them, saying, 'They will respect my son.' 38 But when the tenants saw the son, they said to themselves, 'This is

---

[d] Or *lord*

the heir. Come, let us kill him and take his inheritance.' [39] And they took him and cast him out of the vineyard and killed him. [40] So when the master of the vineyard comes, what will he do to those tenants?" [41] They said to him, "He will bring those evil men to an evil end and lease the vineyard to other tenants, who will give him the fruits in their seasons." [42] Jesus said to them, "Have you never read in the scriptures,

> 'The stone which the builders rejected,
> has become the cornerstone.[a]
> This was the Lord's doing,
> and it is marvelous in our eyes?'[b]

[43] For this reason I say to you that the kingdom of God will be taken from you and given to a people producing its fruits. [44] The one who falls on this stone will be broken in pieces, and on whomever it falls, it will crush him."[c]

[45] And when the chief priests and the Pharisees heard his parables, they knew that he was speaking about them. [46] And although they sought to arrest him, they feared the crowds, because they held him to be a prophet.

The Royal Wedding Feast

22 Once again Jesus spoke to them in parables, saying, [2] "The kingdom of heaven may be compared to a king who held a wedding feast for his son.

---

[a] Literally *the head of the corner* [b] Ps 118:22–23 [c] Some ancient manuscripts lack verse 44

[3] He sent his servants to call those who had been invited to the wedding feast, but they did not want to come. [4] Again, he sent other servants and said, 'Say to those who were called: behold, I have prepared my feast, my bulls and fatted calves have been slaughtered, and all is ready. Come to the wedding feast.' [5] But they ignored it and went away, one to his field, another to his business. [6] And the rest seized his servants and mistreated them and killed them.

[7] "Now the king was angry, so he sent his armies and destroyed those murderers and burned their city. [8] Then he said to his servants, 'The wedding feast is ready, but those who were called were not worthy. [9] Go therefore to the roads leading out of the city and call as many as you can find to the wedding feast.' [10] And those servants went out to the roads, and gathered together everyone they found, both the evil and the good. And the wedding feast was filled with guests. [11] But when the king came in to see the guests at table, he saw there a man who was not wearing a wedding garment. [12] And he said to him, 'Friend, how did you come in here without a wedding garment?' But he was silent. [13] Then the king said to the ministers, 'Bind his feet and hands and cast him into the outer darkness, where there shall be weeping and gnashing of teeth.' [14] For many are called, but few are chosen."

The Question about Paying Taxes to Caesar

[15] Then the Pharisees went and took counsel about how to trap him in his words. [16] And they sent their disciples to him with the Herodians, saying, "Teacher, we know that you are truthful, and that you teach the way of God in truth and are not concerned with anyone's opinion. For you do not regard a person's status. [17] Tell us then, what do you think? Is it lawful to pay the census tax[a] to Caesar or not?" [18] But Jesus knew their evil and said, "Why do you test me, you hypocrites? [19] Show me the coin for the tax." So they brought him a denarius.[b] [20] And he said to them, "Whose image and inscription is this?" [21] They said to him, "Caesar's." Then he said to them, "Therefore render to Caesar the things that are Caesar's, and to God the things that are God's." [22] When they heard it, they marveled, and they left him and went away.

The Question about the Resurrection

[23] On that day, the Sadducees, who say there is no resurrection, came to him and asked him, saying, [24] "Teacher, Moses said, 'If someone dies without having children, his brother shall marry his wife and raise up offspring for his brother.'[c] [25] Now there were seven brothers among us. After the first was married, he died. But having no offspring, he left his wife to his brother.

---

[a] Greek *kensos*, refers to the Latin census or capitation tax collected by the Roman government [b] A Roman silver coin, a common daily wage for a laborer [c] Deut 25:5–6

[26] Likewise, the second also died, and the third, all the way to the seventh. [27] After them all, the wife died. [28] Therefore, in the resurrection, of the seven brothers, whose wife will she be? For they all had her." [29] Jesus answered and said to them, "You are wrong, because you do not know the Scriptures or the power of God. [30] For in the resurrection they neither marry nor are given in marriage, but are like angels in heaven. [31] Regarding the resurrection of the dead, have you not read what was spoken to you by God, [32] 'I am the God of Abraham, the God of Isaac, and the God of Jacob?'[a] He is not the God of the dead, but of the living." [33] And when the crowds heard it, they were astonished at his teaching.

The Question about the Greatest Commandment

[34] But when the Pharisees heard that he had silenced the Sadducees, they gathered together. [35] Then one of them, a lawyer, asked him in order to test him, [36] "Teacher, which is the greatest commandment in the law?" [37] He said to him, "'You shall love the Lord your God with all your heart, with all your soul, and with all your mind.'[b] [38] This is the greatest and first commandment. [39] And a second is like it: 'You shall love your neighbor as yourself.'[c] [40] On these two commandments hang the whole law and the prophets."

---

[a] Exod 3:6 [b] Deut 6:5 [c] Lev 19:18

The Question about the Christ

[41] While the Pharisees were gathered together, Jesus asked them, [42] saying, "What do you think about the Christ? Whose son is he?" They said to him, "David's." [43] He said to them, "How then does David, speaking by the Spirit, call him Lord, saying,

> [44] 'The Lord said to my Lord,
> Sit at my right hand, until I put your
> enemies beneath your feet?'[a]

[45] If then David calls him Lord, how is he his son?" [46] And no one was able to answer him a word, and from that day on no one dared to ask him any more questions.

Whoever Exalts Himself Will Be Humbled

23 Then Jesus spoke to the crowds and to his disciples, [2] saying, "The scribes and Pharisees sit on the seat of Moses. [3] Therefore, do and observe everything they tell you, but do not imitate their works. For they do not practice what they preach. [4] They bind burdens heavy and difficult to carry and lay them on others' shoulders, but they themselves are not willing to lift a finger to move them. [5] They do all their works to be seen by others. For they make their phylacteries[b] wide and their fringes[c] long, [6] and they love the places of honor at banquets, the most prominent seats in the synagogues, [7] the salutations

---

[a] Ps 110:1 [b] Small receptacles containing Scripture verses, strapped to the forehead and left arm during prayer [c] Tassels worn on the four corners of an outer garment as a reminder to keep the commandments; see Num 15:37–40; Deut 22:12

in the markets, and to be called Rabbi[a] by others. [8] But you shall not be called Rabbi, for you have one teacher, and you are all brothers. [9] And call no one your father on earth, for you have one Father, who is in heaven. [10] Nor should you be called teachers, for you have one teacher, the Christ. [11] The greatest among you must be your servant. [12] For whoever exalts himself will be humbled, and whoever humbles himself will be exalted.

Woes Against the Scribes and Pharisees

[13] "But woe to you, scribes and Pharisees, hypocrites! For you lock others out of the kingdom of heaven. You neither enter yourselves, nor do you allow those who would go in to enter.[b]

[15] "Woe to you, scribes and Pharisees, hypocrites! For you travel across sea and dry land to make a single proselyte, and when he becomes one, you make him twice as much a son of Gehenna as yourselves.

[16] "Woe to you, blind guides, who say, 'If anyone swears by the temple, it is nothing. But if anyone swears by the gold of the temple, he is obligated by his oath.' [17] You blind fools! Which is greater, the gold or the temple that makes the gold holy? [18] And you say, 'If anyone swears by the altar, it is nothing, but if anyone swears by the gift upon the altar, he is obligated by his oath.' [19] You blind

---

[a] Hebrew for *my teacher* or *my great one* [b] Some ancient manuscripts include as verse 14: *Woe to you, scribes and Pharisees! You eat up the houses of widows, and for a pretense pray long prayers. For this reason, you will receive the greater condemnation.*

men! Which is greater, the gift or the altar that makes the gift holy? [20] So whoever swears by the altar, swears by it and by everything on it; [21] and whoever swears by the temple, swears by it and by him who dwells in it; [22] and whoever swears by heaven, swears by the throne of God and by him who sits upon it.

[23] "Woe to you, scribes and Pharisees, hypocrites! For you tithe mint and dill and cumin, but have neglected the weightier matters of the law: justice, mercy, and faith. It was necessary to do the former, but without omitting the latter. [24] You blind guides! You strain out a gnat but swallow a camel!

[25] "Woe to you, scribes and Pharisees, hypocrites! For you cleanse the outside of the cup and the dish, but inside you are full of greed and self-indulgence. [26] You blind Pharisee! First cleanse the inside of the cup, so that its outside may also become clean.

[27] "Woe to you, scribes and Pharisees, hypocrites! For you are like whitewashed tombs that appear beautiful on the outside, but inside are filled with the bones of the dead and every uncleanness. [28] So you also on the outside appear righteous to others, but inside you are full of hypocrisy and lawlessness.

[29] "Woe to you, scribes and Pharisees, hypocrites! For you build the graves of the prophets and decorate the

tombs of the righteous, [30] and say, 'If we had lived in the days of our fathers, we would have had no part with them in shedding the blood of the prophets.' [31] Thus you bear witness against yourselves that you are the sons of those who murdered the prophets. [32] Fill up, then, the measure of your fathers. [33] You serpents, you brood of vipers! How will you escape from the judgment of Gehenna? [34] Therefore behold, I send you prophets and wise men and scribes. Some of them you will kill and crucify, and some of them you will flog in your synagogues and pursue from city to city, [35] so that upon you may come all the righteous blood poured out upon the earth—from the blood of Abel the just to the blood of Zechariah, the son of Barachiah, whom you murdered between the temple and the altar. [36] Amen, I say to you, all these things shall come upon this generation.

Jesus Laments Over Jerusalem

[37] "O Jerusalem, Jerusalem, who kills the prophets and stones those who are sent to her! How often I would have gathered your children like a hen gathers her young beneath her wings, but you would not. [38] Behold, your house is left to you, desolate.[a] [39] For I say to you, you will not see me again until you say, 'Blessed is he who comes in the name of the Lord!'"[b]

---

[a] Jer 22:5 [b] Ps 118:26

The Destruction of the Temple

24 And Jesus left the temple and was going away, when his disciples came to point out to him the buildings of the temple. [2] But he answered and said to them, "Do you not see all these things? Amen, I say to you, there will not be left here one stone upon another that will not be thrown down." [3] And as he sat on the Mount of Olives, the disciples came to him privately, saying, "Tell us, when will these things take place? And what will be the sign of your coming and of the end of the age?"

The Beginning of the Birth Pangs

[4] And Jesus answered and said to them, "See that no one deceives you, [5] for many will come in my name, saying, 'I am the Christ,' and they will deceive many. [6] You will hear of wars and rumors of wars; see that you are not alarmed. For all this must take place, but the end is not yet. [7] For nation will rise against nation, and kingdom against kingdom, and there will be famines and earthquakes in various places. [8] All these things are the beginning of the birth pangs. [9] Then they will hand you over to tribulation and kill you, and you will be hated by all nations because of my name. [10] Then many will fall away, and they will betray one another and hate

one another. [11] Many false prophets will arise and deceive many. [12] And because lawlessness will increase, the love of many will grow cold. [13] But the one who endures to the end shall be saved. [14] And this gospel of the kingdom will be preached in the whole world, as a witness to all the Gentiles, and then the end will come.

The Great Tribulation

[15] "Therefore, when you see the abomination of desolation spoken of through Daniel the prophet standing in the holy place, let the reader understand.[d] [16] Then let those who are in Judea flee to the mountains. [17] Let the one who is on his housetop not go down to take what is in his house, [18] and let the one who is in his field not turn back to take his cloak. [19] Woe to those who are pregnant and nursing in those days!

[20] "But pray that your flight may not take place in winter or on a Sabbath. [21] For then there will be great tribulation such as has not taken place from the beginning of the world until now, nor ever will take place again. [22] And if those days had not been shortened, no one would be saved. But for the sake of the elect, those days will be shortened. [23] Then if anyone says to you, 'Look, here is the Christ!' or 'There he is!' do not believe it. [24] For false christs and false prophets will arise, and they

---

[d] Dan 9:27; 11:31; 12:11

will perform great signs and wonders in order to deceive, if possible, even the elect. [25] Behold, I have foretold this to you. [26] Therefore, if they say to you, 'Look, he is in the desert!' do not go out. Or, 'Look, he is in the inner rooms!' do not believe it. [27] For as the lightning comes from the east and flashes as far as the west, so will be the coming of the Son of Man. [28] Wherever the corpse is, there the eagles will gather.

The Coming of the Son of Man

[29] "And immediately after the tribulation of those days, the sun will be darkened and the moon will not give her light, and the stars will fall from heaven and the powers of heaven will be shaken. [30] Then the sign of the Son of Man will appear in heaven, and all the tribes of the earth will mourn, and they will see the Son of Man coming upon the clouds of heaven with power and great glory.[d] [31] And he will send forth his angels with the sound of a great trumpet, and they will gather his elect from the four winds, from one end of the heavens to the other.

[32] "From the fig tree learn the parable: when its branch becomes tender and puts forth leaves, you know that summer is near. [33] So likewise, when you see all these things, know that he is near, even at the gates. [34] Amen, I say to you, this generation shall not pass away

---

[d] Dan 7:13–14

until all these things take place. [35] Heaven and earth shall pass away, but my words shall never pass away. [36] But about that day and hour no one knows, neither the angels of heaven, nor the Son, but only the Father.

[37] "For just as it was in the days of Noah, so it will be at the coming of the Son of Man. [38] For as in those days before the flood, they were eating and drinking, marrying and giving in marriage, until the day that Noah entered the ark, [39] and they did not know until the flood came and swept them all away, so too will be the coming of the Son of Man. [40] Then two men will be in the field; one will be taken, and one will be left. [41] Two women will be grinding at the mill; one will be taken, and one will be left.

The Thief in the Night

[42] "Stay awake, therefore, for you do not know what day your Lord is coming. [43] But know this, that if the master of the house had known in what watch of the night the thief would come, he would have stayed awake and not have let his house be broken into. [44] Therefore, you also must be ready, for the Son of Man is coming at an hour you do not expect.

The Faithful Servant

[45] "Who then is the faithful and wise servant, whom his master has appointed over his household to give them

food at the proper time? [46] Blessed is that servant whom his master will find so doing when he comes. [47] Amen, I say to you, he will appoint him over all his possessions. [48] But if that evil servant says in his heart, 'My master is delayed,' [49] and he begins to strike his fellow servants and to eat and drink with the drunken, [50] the master of that servant will come on a day when he does not expect and at an hour that he does not know, [51] and he shall cut him in two and put him with the hypocrites, where there shall be weeping and gnashing of teeth.

The Ten Virgins

25 "Then the kingdom of heaven will be compared to ten virgins who took their lamps and went out to meet the bridegroom. [2] Five of them were foolish, and five were wise. [3] For the foolish took their lamps but did not take oil with them, [4] while the wise took flasks of oil with their lamps. [5] While the bridegroom was delayed, they all became drowsy and slept. [6] At midnight, there was a shout, 'Behold, the bridegroom! Go out to meet him.' [7] Then all those virgins rose and lit their lamps. [8] The foolish said to the wise, 'Give us some of your oil, since our lamps have gone out.' [9] But the wise answered and said, 'No, for there will not be enough for us and for you. Rather, go to the merchants and buy some for yourselves.' [10] And while they were going to buy some,

the bridegroom came, and those who were ready went in with him to the wedding feast, and the door was locked. [11] Afterward the rest of the virgins also came, saying, 'Lord, Lord, open to us!' [12] But he answered and said, 'Amen, I say to you, I do not know you.' [13] Stay awake, therefore, for you do not know the day or the hour.

The Talents

[14] "For it is like a man going away on a journey, who called his servants and entrusted his possessions to them. [15] To one he gave five talents,[a] to another, two talents, and to another, one talent—to each according to his ability. Immediately he set out on his journey. [16] The one who had received the five talents went and traded with them and made five more. [17] Likewise, the one who had received the two talents made two more. [18] But the one who had received the one talent went away, dug a hole in the ground, and hid his master's money. [19] Now after a long time, the master of those servants came and settled accounts with them. [20] And the one who had received the five talents came and brought five more talents, saying, 'Master, you entrusted five talents to me. See, I have made five more talents.' [21] His master said to him, 'Well done, good and faithful servant. You have been faithful with a few things; I will put you in charge of many. Enter into

[a] Greek *talanton*; a single talent was worth about 6,000 days' wages for a laborer

the joy of your master.' [22] The one who had received the two talents also came and said, 'Master, you entrusted two talents to me. See, I have made two more talents.' [23] His master said to him, 'Well done, good and faithful servant. You have been faithful with a few things; I will put you in charge of many. Enter into the joy of your master.' [24] Then the one who had received the one talent came and said, 'Master, I knew you were a hard man, reaping where you have not sown, and gathering where you have not scattered. [25] So I was afraid and went and hid your talent in the ground. Here, have what is yours.' [26] His master answered and said to him, 'You evil and lazy servant! You knew that I reap where I have not sown and gather where I have not scattered? [27] Then you should have given my money to the lenders, and at my coming I would have recovered what was mine with interest. [28] Therefore, take the talent away from him and give it to the one who has ten talents. [29] For to everyone who has, more will be given, and he will have in abundance. But from the one who does not have, even what he has will be taken away. [30] And cast the unprofitable servant into the outer darkness, where there shall be weeping and gnashing of teeth.'

The Sheep and the Goats

[31] "When the Son of Man comes in his glory and all the angels with him, then he will sit upon his throne of

glory. [32] And all nations will be gathered before him, and he will separate them one from another, like a shepherd separates the sheep from the goats. [33] And he will place the sheep at his right hand and the goats at his left. [34] Then the King will say to those at his right hand, 'Come, you blessed of my Father, inherit the kingdom prepared for you from the foundation of the world. [35] For I was hungry and you gave me food, I was thirsty and you gave me drink, I was a stranger and you took me in, [36] I was naked and you clothed me, I was sick and you visited me, I was in prison and you came to me.' [37] Then the righteous will answer him, saying, 'Lord, when did we see you hungry and feed you, or thirsty and give you drink? [38] When did we see you a stranger and take you in, or naked and clothe you? [39] And when did we see you sick or in prison and visit you?' [40] And the King will answer and say to them, 'Amen, I say to you, whatever you did to one of the least of these my brothers, you did it to me.' [41] Then he will also say to those at his left hand, 'Depart from me, you accursed, into the eternal fire prepared for the devil and his angels. [42] For I was hungry and you gave me no food, I was thirsty and you gave me no drink, [43] I was a stranger and you did not take me in, I was naked and you did not clothe me, I was sick and in prison and you did not visit me.' [44] Then they will also answer him, saying, 'Lord, when did we see you hungry or thirsty or a stranger or naked or sick or in prison, and not minister to you?' [45] Then he will answer them, saying, 'Amen, I say to you, whatever you did not do to one of the least of these, you did not do to me.' [46] And these will go away to eternal punishment, but the righteous to eternal life."

The Passion of Jesus Christ

26 Now when Jesus had finished all these words, he said to his disciples, [2] "You know that after two days Passover is coming, and the Son of Man will be handed over to be crucified."

[3] Then the chief priests and the elders of the people gathered together in the courtyard of the high priest, who was called Caiaphas. [4] And they took counsel that they might arrest Jesus by deceit and kill him. [5] But they said, "Not at the feast, lest there be a riot among the people."

The Anointing at Bethany

[6] Now when Jesus was in Bethany in the house of Simon the leper, [7] a woman came to him with an alabaster jar of very costly ointment. And she poured it on his head as he reclined at table. [8] But when his disciples saw it, they were indignant, saying, "Why this waste? [9] For this ointment could have been sold for a large sum and given

to the poor." [10] When Jesus perceived it, he said to them, "Why do you trouble the woman? She has done a good work for me. [11] For you always have the poor with you, but you will not always have me. [12] When she poured this ointment on my body, she did it for my burial. [13] Amen, I say to you, wherever this gospel is preached in the whole world, what she has done will be spoken of, in memory of her."

Judas and the Thirty Pieces of Silver

[14] Then one of the twelve, who was called Judas Iscariot, went to the chief priests [15] and said, "What are you willing to give me if I hand him over to you?" And they agreed to give him thirty pieces of silver. [16] And from that time, he sought an opportunity to betray him.

The Last Supper

[17] Now on the first day of Unleavened Bread, the disciples came to Jesus, saying, "Where do you want us to prepare for you to eat the Passover?" [18] And he said, "Go into the city to a certain person and say to him, 'The Teacher says, My time is at hand. I will keep the Passover at your house with my disciples.'" [19] And the disciples did as Jesus had directed them, and they prepared the Passover.

[20] Now when it was evening, he reclined at table with the twelve. [21] And while they were eating, he said, "Amen,

I say to you, one of you will betray me." [22] And they were exceedingly sorrowful, and each one of them began to say to him, "Surely not I, Lord?" [23] And he answered and said, "The one who dips his hand in the dish with me will betray me. [24] The Son of Man goes as it is written of him, but woe to that man by whom the Son of Man is betrayed! It would have been better for that man if he had never been born." [25] Then Judas, his betrayer, answered and said, "Surely not I, Rabbi?" He said to him, "You have said it."

[26] And as they were eating, Jesus took bread, said the blessing, broke it, and gave it to the disciples, and said, "Take, eat; this is my body." [27] And he took a cup, and giving thanks, he gave it to them, saying, "Drink from it, all of you. [28] For this is my blood of the covenant,[a] which is poured out for many for the forgiveness of sins. [29] But I say to you, from now on, I will not drink of this fruit of the vine until that day when I drink it new with you in the kingdom of my Father."

Strike the Shepherd and the Sheep Will Be Scattered

[30] And after singing a hymn, they went out to the Mount of Olives. [31] Then Jesus said to them, "This very night you will all fall away because of me. For it is written, 'I will strike the shepherd, and the sheep of the flock will

---

[a] Some ancient manuscripts have *new covenant*

be scattered.'[d] [32] But after I am raised up, I will go before you into Galilee." [33] But Peter answered and said to him, "If all fall away because of you, I will never fall away." [34] Jesus said to him, "Amen, I say to you, on this very night, before the cock crows, you will deny me three times." [35] Peter said to him, "Even if I must die with you, I will never deny you." And all the disciples said likewise.

The Agony in Gethsemane

[36] Then Jesus came with them to a place called Gethsemane and said to the disciples, "Sit here, while I go over there and pray." [37] And he took Peter and the two sons of Zebedee with him, and he began to be sorrowful and distressed. [38] Then he said to them, "My soul is very sorrowful, even unto death. Remain here, and keep watch with me." [39] And going a short distance away, he fell on his face and prayed, saying, "My Father, if it is possible, let this cup pass from me; yet, not as I will, but as you will." [40] And he came to the disciples and found them sleeping, and he said to Peter, "So you could not keep watch with me one hour? [41] Watch and pray that you may not enter into temptation. The spirit is willing, but the flesh is weak." [42] He went away again a second time and prayed, saying, "My Father, if it is not possible for this cup to pass from me unless I drink it, your will be done." [43] And he came and found them sleeping again, for their eyelids

---

[d] Zech 13:7

were heavy. [44] And he left them and went away once more and prayed a third time, saying the same words. [45] Then he came to the disciples and said to them, "Are you still sleeping and taking your rest? Behold, the hour has come, and the Son of Man is betrayed into the hands of sinners. [46] Rise, let us be going. See, my betrayer is at hand."

Jesus is Arrested

[47] While he was still speaking, behold, Judas, one of the twelve, came with a great crowd with swords and clubs, from the chief priests and elders of the people. [48] Now his betrayer gave them a sign, saying, "Whoever I kiss is the one; arrest him." [49] And immediately he came to Jesus, and said, "Hail, Rabbi!" And he kissed him. [50] And Jesus said to him, "Friend, why are you here?" Then they came and laid hands on Jesus and arrested him. [51] And behold, one of those with Jesus stretched out his hand, drew his sword, struck the servant of the high priest, and cut off his ear.

[52] Then Jesus said to him, "Put your sword back in its place! For all who take up the sword will perish by the sword. [53] Do you think I am not able to call upon my Father, and he will at once send me more than twelve legions of angels? [54] But how would the scriptures be fulfilled, which say that it must happen this way?" [55] In that hour Jesus said to the crowds, "Have you come out with swords and clubs to seize me, as though I were a

robber? Day after day I sat teaching in the temple, and you did not arrest me. [56] But all this has taken place so that the writings of the prophets might be fulfilled." Then all the disciples deserted him and fled.

Jesus Before the Sanhedrin

[57] Then those who arrested Jesus led him away to Caiaphas the high priest, where the scribes and the elders were gathered. [58] But Peter followed him from a distance as far as the courtyard of the high priest, and he went inside and sat with the servants, to see the end.

[59] Now the chief priests and the whole Sanhedrin were seeking false testimony against Jesus in order to put him to death, [60] but they found none, though many false witnesses came forward. Finally, two came forward [61] and said, "This man said, 'I am able to destroy the temple of God and to build it in three days.'" [62] And the high priest rose up and said to him, "Have you no answer to what these men testify against you?" [63] But Jesus was silent. And the high priest said to him, "I adjure you by the living God, tell us if you are the Christ, the Son of God." [64] Jesus said to him, "You have said it. But I say to you,

From now on, you will see the Son of Man
seated at the right hand of Power
and coming on the clouds of heaven."[a]

---

[a] Ps 110:1; Dan 7:13

[65] Then the high priest tore his garments, saying, "He has blasphemed! Why do we still need witnesses? See now, you have heard his blasphemy. [66] What is your verdict?" They answered and said, "He deserves death." [67] Then they spat in his face, and beat him, and struck him, [68] saying, "Prophesy to us, you Christ! Who is it that struck you?"

Peter Denies Jesus Three Times

[69] Now Peter was sitting outside in the courtyard. And a servant girl came to him, saying, "You also were with Jesus the Galilean." [70] But he denied it before them all, saying, "I do not know what you are talking about." [71] And when he went out to the gateway, another servant girl saw him and said to those who were there, "This man was with Jesus the Nazarene." [72] And again he denied it with an oath, "I do not know the man!" [73] After a little while, those who were standing by came and said to Peter, "Truly you also are one of them, for your accent gives you away!" [74] Then he began to curse and to swear, "I do not know the man!" And immediately the cock crowed. [75] Then Peter remembered the word Jesus had spoken: "Before the cock crows, you will deny me three times." And he went out and wept bitterly.

The Sanhedrin Meets Again

27 When it was morning, all the chief priests and elders of the people took counsel against Jesus to put him to death. [2] And when they had bound him, they led him away and handed him over to Pilate the governor.

The Death of Judas

[3] When Judas, his betrayer, saw that he was condemned, he regretted what he had done and returned the thirty pieces of silver to the chief priests and elders, [4] saying, "I have sinned by betraying innocent blood." And they said, "What is that to us? See to it yourself!" [5] And he threw down the pieces of silver in the temple and departed, and he went away and hanged himself. [6] And the chief priests took the silver pieces and said, "It is not lawful to put this in the temple treasury, since it is blood money." [7] So they took counsel and used them to buy the Potter's field as a burial place for strangers. [8] Therefore that field has been called the Field of Blood to this day. [9] Then was fulfilled what was spoken through Jeremiah the prophet, "And they took the thirty pieces of silver, the price of him on whom a price had been placed by some of the sons of Israel. [10] And they gave them for the Potter's field, just as the Lord ordered me."[a]

---

[a] Jer 32:7–9; Zech 11:12

Pilate Questions Jesus

[11] Now Jesus stood before the governor, and the governor asked him, saying, "Are you indeed the King of the Jews?" And Jesus said to him, "You say so." [12] And when he was accused by the chief priests and elders, he gave no answer. [13] Then Pilate said to him, "Do you not hear how many things they testify against you?" [14] But he gave no answer to him, not even to one word, so that the governor marveled greatly.

Barabbas and Jesus

[15] Now at the feast the governor was accustomed to release one prisoner for the crowd, whomever they wanted. [16] And they had at that time a notorious prisoner called Barabbas.[a] [17] So when they were gathered together, Pilate said to them, "Whom do you want me to release for you? Barabbas?[b] Or Jesus, who is called Christ?" [18] For he knew they had handed him over because of envy.

[19] While he was sitting on the judgment seat, his wife sent word to him, saying, "Have nothing to do with that righteous man, for I have suffered many things today in a dream because of him." [20] But the chief priests and elders persuaded the crowds to ask for Barabbas and destroy Jesus. [21] The governor answered and said to them, "Which of the two do you want me to release for you?"

---

[a] Some ancient manuscripts have *Jesus Barabbas* [b] Some ancient manuscripts have *Jesus Barabbas*

They said, "Barabbas!" [22] Pilate said to them, "What then shall I do with Jesus who is called Christ?" They all said, "Let him be crucified!" [23] But the governor said, "Why, what evil has he done?" But they shouted all the louder, saying, "Let him be crucified!"

[24] When Pilate saw that he was accomplishing nothing, but rather that a riot was breaking out, he took water and washed his hands in front of the crowd, saying, "I am innocent of this man's blood. See to it yourselves!" [25] Then all the people answered and said, "His blood be upon us and upon our children." [26] Then he released Barabbas to them. And after he had Jesus scourged, he handed him over to be crucified.

The Crowning with Thorns

[27] Then the soldiers of the governor took Jesus into the praetorium[a] and gathered the whole cohort[b] to him. [28] They stripped him and put a scarlet robe around him. [29] And weaving a crown of thorns, they placed it on his head and put a reed in his right hand. And they knelt before him and mocked him, saying, "Hail, King of the Jews!" [30] And they spit on him and took the reed and struck him on the head. [31] And after they had mocked him, they stripped him of the robe, put his own garments on him, and led him away to crucify him.

---

[a] The Roman governor's residence [b] Greek *speira*, one tenth of a Roman legion or about 600 soldiers

The Crucifixion

[32] As they came out, they found a man of Cyrene named Simon. This man they forced to carry his cross. [33] And when they came to a place called Golgotha, which means "the Place of the Skull," [34] they gave him wine mixed with gall to drink. But when he tasted it, he would not drink it. [35] And when they had crucified him, they divided his garments by casting lots. [36] And they sat down and kept watch over him there. [37] And they placed over his head the charge against him, which read, "This is Jesus, the King of the Jews."

[38] Then two robbers[a] were crucified with him, one on his right hand and one on his left. [39] And those who passed by blasphemed him, wagging their heads [40] and saying, "You who would destroy the temple and build it in three days, save yourself! If you are the Son of God, then come down from the cross!" [41] In the same way, the chief priests also mocked him along with the scribes and elders, saying, [42] "He saved others; he cannot save himself! If he is the King of Israel, let him come down from the cross now, and we will believe in him. [43] He trusted in God; let him deliver him now, if he wants him! For he said, 'I am the Son of God.'" [44] The robbers who were crucified with him also reviled him in the same way.

---

[a] Or *rebels*

The Death of Jesus

[45] Now from the sixth hour,[a] there was darkness over all the earth[b] until the ninth hour.[c] [46] And about the ninth hour, Jesus cried out with a loud voice, saying, "*Eli, Eli, lema sabachthani?*" that is, "My God, my God, why have you forsaken me?"[d] [47] When some of those standing there heard it, they said, "This man is calling for Elijah." [48] And immediately one of them ran and took a sponge, filled it with sour wine, put it on a reed, and gave it to him to drink.[e] [49] But the rest said, "Wait! Let us see if Elijah will come to save him." [50] And when Jesus had cried out again with a loud voice, he gave up his spirit.

[51] And behold, the veil of the temple was torn in two from top to bottom. The earth shook, and the rocks were split. [52] The tombs were also opened, and many bodies of the saints who had fallen asleep were raised. [53] And after his resurrection, they came out of the tombs and went into the holy city and appeared to many. [54] Now when the centurion and those with him, who were keeping watch over Jesus, saw the earthquake and what took place, they were terrified and said, "Truly this was the Son of God!"

[55] And many women who had followed Jesus from Galilee and ministered to him were there, looking on from a distance. [56] Among them were Mary Magdalene, Mary the mother of James and Joseph, and the mother of the sons of Zebedee.

---

[a] Noon [b] Or *all the land* [c] 3pm [d] Ps 22:1 [e] Some ancient manuscripts include *Now someone else took a spear and pierced his side, and water and blood flowed out.*

The Burial of Jesus

[57] When it was evening, there came a rich man of Arimathea named Joseph, who was himself a disciple of Jesus. [58] This man went to Pilate and asked him for the body of Jesus. Then Pilate commanded it to be given. [59] And taking the body, Joseph wrapped it in a clean linen shroud [60] and placed it in his own new tomb, which he had cut in the rock. And he rolled a great stone to the door of the tomb and departed. [61] And Mary Magdalene was there, and the other Mary, sitting opposite the tomb.

The Sealing of the Tomb

[62] On the next day, after the day of Preparation,[a] the chief priests and the Pharisees gathered before Pilate, [63] saying, "We remember, lord,[b] how that deceiver said while he was still living, 'After three days I will rise.' [64] Therefore command that the grave be made secure until the third day, lest his disciples come and steal the body and say to the people, 'He is risen from the dead.' Then the last deception will be worse than the first." [65] Pilate said to them, "You have a guard of soldiers. Go, and make it as secure as you can." [66] So they went with the guard and secured the tomb, putting a seal on the stone.

---

[a] Or *Friday*, the day before the Jewish Sabbath [b] Greek *kyrios*

The Resurrection of Jesus

28 Now after the Sabbath, at dawn on the first day of the week, Mary Magdalene and the other Mary came to see the tomb. [2] And behold, there was a great earthquake; for an angel of the Lord, descending from heaven, came and rolled away the stone and sat on it. [3] His appearance was like lightning, and his clothing was white as snow. [4] For fear of him, the guards were shaken and became like dead men. [5] But the angel said to the women, "Do not fear, for I know that you seek Jesus who was crucified. [6] He is not here; for he is risen, just as he said. Come, see the place where he lay. [7] Then go quickly and tell his disciples, 'He is risen from the dead. And behold, he is going before you into Galilee. There you will see him.' Behold, I have told you." [8] And they departed quickly from the tomb with fear and great joy, and they ran to tell his disciples. [9] And behold, Jesus met them, saying, "Greetings!" And they came and embraced his feet and worshiped him. [10] Then Jesus said to them, "Do not fear. Go, tell my brothers to go to Galilee. There they will see me."

The Story Told by the Soldiers

[11] Now as they were going, behold, some of the guard went into the city and told the chief priests everything that had taken place. [12] And when they gathered with the elders and had taken counsel, they gave a large sum of money to the soldiers [13] and said, "Say this, 'His disciples

came by night and stole the body while we were sleeping.' [14] And if the governor hears of this, we will satisfy him and keep you free from worry." [15] So they took the silver and did as they were instructed. And this story has been spread among Jews to this day.

The Great Commission

[16] Then the eleven disciples went into Galilee to the mountain to which Jesus had directed them. [17] And when they saw him, they worshiped him, but some doubted. [18] And Jesus came and spoke to them, saying, "All authority in heaven and on earth has been given to me. [19] Go therefore and make disciples of all nations, baptizing them in the name of the Father, and of the Son, and of the Holy Spirit, [20] and teaching them to observe everything I have commanded you. And behold, I am with you always, until the end of the age."

HOW TO PRAY WITH SCRIPTURE

Elizabeth Klein

We can talk to God at any time, because he is our loving Father, because Christ has pledged to be with us always even to the end of the age (Matthew 28:20), and because the Holy Spirit has been sent to dwell within us (Ephesians 3:16; Romans 5:5). Yet we all recognize from our own relationships that the better we come to know someone, the more easily we are able to speak with him. And if we come to know someone very well, we can even rest in silence with him and be completely comfortable. Coming to know God in the Scriptures is coming to know more deeply the one to whom we are speaking, and to develop a better language for speaking with him.

The Bible's guidance for our life of prayer is a great gift. After all, it is not always easy to pray or to know how to pray. Even the disciples asked Jesus to teach them how to pray, and he responded by giving them the Our Father (see Matthew 6:9–13) which is still the first prayer many of us learn as children, and it is the prayer that we say together as the People of God every Sunday. The Our Father shows us what to ask God for: for his name to be first before all else ("hallowed be your name"), for his rule to be ours ("your kingdom come, your will be done"), for our daily needs, both bodily and spiritual ("give us this day our daily bread"), for forgiveness and the grace to forgive ("forgive us our trespasses as we forgive those who trespass against us") and for both bodily and spiritual protection ("lead us not into temptation, but deliver us from evil"). So even if you do not think of yourself as someone who prays with Scripture, in our Catholic devotions and through the liturgy, you are already praying with the Bible.

The way in which the Church has traditionally practiced praying with the Scriptures and listening for God's voice in them is called *lectio divina*, which means "divine reading." This practice is traditionally understood to have four stages: reading, meditating, praying, and contemplating.

The first step in *lectio divina* is the one from which the whole process gets its name: careful, slow reading of Scripture. Learning to read in this way takes practice, especially in our present time. Unlike scanning an email or text message, *lectio divina* calls for sustained attention, for the savoring of details, and for the turning over and questioning of phrases. Take a moment to collect yourself before you begin reading, and to ask God to illuminate your mind as you read. If you find yourself reading too quickly, go back to the beginning and start again. You can ask questions about the passage, remind yourself of the people mentioned (Who are they? What are they doing?) and search out the meaning of unknown words and phrases. Too often, we pass over words with which we are unfamiliar. Notice interesting turns of phrases, images, and so on. If it is helpful for you, you could imagine a biblical scene with all of its details and place yourself within it.

By doing careful reading, one is able to move to the next step of *lectio divina*—meditation. If we took the time to notice the details of a passage, the images it uses, or if we imagined ourselves within a biblical scene, deeper questions of meaning will arise. What is the passage really trying to say? What does the passage tell me about God? And how does the passage tell me about myself? How is God speaking to me in the passage? This process may not necessarily yield as many answers as it does questions, nor is it a rigorous analysis of a passage. Rather, we are allowing space for the Holy Spirit to work in our hearts.

Now that we have read God's Word and meditated on it, we have something to talk to God about; and so the third step of *lectio* is prayer. Bring to God what you have found in his Word. If you have found some message therein upon which you need to act, pray to God for the grace to do so. If you have been perplexed, bring your questions to God and talk it over with him. If you have found some consolation or the sweetness of an insight you did not have before, thank God for it. Prayer is supposed to be a conversation, and your reading and meditation will give you some good conversation starters. Sometimes in this process we may feel peace, like Mary sitting at the feet of Christ and doing the one thing necessary. At other times, we might feel like Jacob wrestling with the angel of God. But such difficult moments come and go in any relationship of love, and we are the stronger for them.

The last stage of *lectio divina* is contemplation. In plain English, the words "meditation" and "contemplation" are similar, so it may seem difficult to make any sense of the difference between them. But if we think about how we use these words, meditation is usually an activity that requires some effort on our part, some concentration and intention. Contemplation, however, is something that we can be lost in—as in the expression "lost in thought." That is how these two stages are also distinguished in *lectio divina*. Contemplation cannot be achieved by any force of our will, but it is God's response to us. It is an experience of being with God that is a gift, and that transcends normal human thinking. Contemplation is like being silent in God's presence and in complete peace, a moment of rest and love that is beyond words. So, although contemplation in some ways defies a definition in words, it is known to us to some degree by even common human experience. We have all had moments of quiet joy, peace, and love in the presence of a child, friend, or spouse, and they are very difficult to describe—and perhaps we can even recall some such moment in our lives where we felt that way in the presence of God too. These moments of contemplation may not follow *lectio divina,* just as we cannot orchestrate those precious moments of love in human life, but we know that by reading, meditating, and praying we create the right conditions for such a moment to happen, and for us to receive God's grace in them.

When we learn to pray with the Bible, we open ourselves up for conversation with God and allow ourselves to be challenged by his Word, which can often be demanding and difficult to understand. But we Catholics do not need to be afraid to pray with Scripture nor to avoid it on account of those difficulties. We can look to great saints and Doctors of the Church for an example of how to pray and for help in understanding the Scriptures. We can attend Bible studies at our parish and be attentive to homilies that expound the Word of God. There is no reason to be intimidated by praying with Scripture: it is a training in humility, an exercise in listening to God, and a discipline of the whole Church.

THE GOSPEL OF MATTHEW

MEDITATION PROMPTS

MATTHEW 1

The genealogy of Jesus points us to the mystery of the Incarnation. It reminds us that God has entered the bloodstream of the human race. Think about the magnitude of God's love revealed in this mystery. He did not have to become one of us in order to save us, but he chose to draw close to us in this way.

Imagine yourself in Joseph's situation and marvel at the level of trust that was asked of him. Consider that God sometimes uses perplexing circumstances to invite you into deeper faith. Contemplate the ways that God normally speaks to you and leads you to fulfill his plan in your life.

MATTHEW 2

Think about the glaring contrast between Herod, who is agitated and angry, and the magi, who bow in worship before the infant King and offer him precious gifts. Identify some of your own treasures that could be made an offering to Jesus.

Joseph is shown to be a righteous man, not least by his prompt obedience to God's commands. How do you measure up to this standard? When you realize that the Lord wants something of you, do you hesitate and drag your feet, or do you respond quickly and decisively?

MATTHEW 3

John the Baptist prepares the way for Jesus by calling God's people to repent. Think about an area of your life where repentance and detachment from sin is needed. Ask the Lord to help you bear fruit that is worthy of repentance.

The Baptism of Jesus teaches us about our own Baptism, showing that God calls us beloved sons and daughters when he gives us his Spirit. How does being a child of God make a difference in the way you serve him and relate to him?

MATTHEW 4

Consider how Jesus defeated the temptations of the devil. Consider too his weapon of choice. What does this tell us about Scripture and its role in living a victorious Christian life?

The call of the first disciples is one of Jesus' most spectacular miracles. It was comparatively easy for him to heal the body of sickness or to silence the wind and the waves of the sea. A greater feat was winning the souls of sinful and selfish people to become lifelong disciples. Marvel at the captivating power of Christ's call and Christ's grace, which together draw us to a new way of life.

MATTHEW 5

Take a moment to linger over the eight Beatitudes. Call to mind one of the Church's canonized saints whose life reflects these Christian ideals in concrete ways. Allow yourself to be challenged by these high standards, and ask the Lord for the gift of a greater adherence to his teaching.

Jesus calls disciples to imitate the love of the heavenly Father, which extends even to enemies. Pause over this point in silence and be amazed at the vastness of God's goodness to all, the deserving and undeserving alike. This kind of love, according to Jesus, lies at the heart of spiritual perfection.

MATTHEW 6

Jesus insists that our heavenly Father sees in secret and rewards those who serve him in secret. Accept this as a challenge to develop an interior life of prayer and spiritual discipline that is kept hidden from all except the Lord.

Jesus challenges us to put God's kingdom and righteousness before other human priorities, including our basic needs for food and clothing. Allow the implication of Jesus' teaching to sink in: the needs of the human soul are even greater than the needs of the body. Recognizing this truth is vital to living an authentic Christian life.

MATTHEW 7

The life of prayer is a life of asking, seeking, and knocking for the good gifts of the Father. Ultimately, however,

Jesus lifts our gaze above these gifts to the incomparable goodness of the Giver. Ponder the words "how much more" in Jesus' saying.

Reflect on the Parable of the Two Builders. In what does true wisdom consist, according to Jesus? What are some of the howling winds and torrents of rain that test the foundations of our lives?

MATTHEW 8

The words of the centurion are taken up into the words of the Eucharistic Liturgy: "Lord, I am not worthy that you should enter under my roof, but only say the word..." Be amazed at this tremendous mystery. Holy Communion brings Jesus under the shelter of your soul to restore its life and health once again!

Jesus denies a man's request to bury his father before becoming a disciple. Honoring one's father and mother is a sacred duty enshrined in the Ten Commandments. What does this denial say about the level of commitment that Jesus demands for his followers? What does it say about Jesus himself?

MATTHEW 9

The Healing of the Paralytic is a double miracle that restores a man's body and soul. The connection between these two healings implies that sin is a kind of spiritual paralysis that cripples our ability to live as God intends. Contemplate this in light of the Sacrament of Reconciliation and its purpose.

Jesus is ridiculed for claiming that a dead girl was sleeping. But consider what he is teaching us by speaking in this way. Jesus is reminding us that the death of the body is a temporary situation, not a permanent one. It is a prelude to resurrection. Death and corruption do not have the last word, for Scripture reveals that God will raise the dead to live again!

MATTHEW 10

Jesus promises that the Holy Spirit will help those who bear witness to the gospel in the face of opposition. This reminds us of our need for God's grace, especially when we are asked to do what is frighteningly difficult. Thank Jesus for his promise to supply what we lack when our witness to the gospel matters most.

Every disciple must take up his cross to be worthy of Christ. This saying has lost much of its punch in our modern world. But consider how the words would have sounded in a world where crucifixion was a brutal reality of life. They speak of heroic suffering in imitation of Jesus in his Passion. Have we really come to grips with Jesus' words and allowed them to challenge our chronic human desire to avoid suffering at all costs?

MATTHEW 11

Jesus speaks mysterious words when he says that "the violent seize" the kingdom of heaven "by force." An ancient tradition of the Church understands this as a reference to asceticism (fasting and other forms of spiritual discipline) as exemplified in John the Baptist. Consider how the "violence" of self-denial frees you from the tyranny of selfish desires and helps you to seize hold of the kingdom.

The Father reveals the hidden truths of the kingdom to infants rather than the wise. Ponder what it means to be an infant in this sense. What makes little children different from educated adults when it comes to receiving the truth of the gospel?

MATTHEW 12

The Sabbath is a sacred day of rest, a day when unnecessary labors are set aside. It should grab our attention, then, that Jesus chooses the Sabbath as the most suitable day to heal the sick and the crippled. Jesus is not breaking the Sabbath; rather, he is conferring its blessings on others. Consider that he is giving rest to the weary by removing their heaviest burdens.

Jesus does not hide from us the dark reality of spiritual warfare. His exorcisms and teachings about the devil are proof of this. Remind yourself that Jesus, the divine Son, is stronger than the "strong man," the ruler of demons. He has the power to bind Beelzebul (Satan) and the power to release his captives.

MATTHEW 13

The Parable of the Sower illustrates people's diverse responses to Jesus. It may be reassuring to think of yourself as the good soil, but can we honestly say that we've never received the Word with joy, only to find our enthusiasm cooling at a later time? Can we honestly say that the thorns of worldly concerns have never threatened our spiritual commitments? What makes the good soil consistently receptive to growth?

Reflect on the Parable of the Weeds and the Wheat. Ask yourself why the Lord allows them to grow together until the harvest. Does it point to God's mercy in giving the weeds ample time for repentance? Does it suggest that God affords the wheat ample opportunity to pray and sacrifice for all who claim membership in the Church?

MATTHEW 14

In the Feeding of the Five Thousand, Jesus gave the multiplied bread to the disciples, and the disciples in turn gave it to the crowds. Jesus could have distributed the loaves by himself, but he chose to involve his disciples in this work. Ponder this detail in relation to the Eucharist and the ministerial priesthood.

Jesus manifests the inner mystery of his divinity by walking on the sea. Take particular note of how the disciples respond to this revelation. At first, they cry out in fear; but once Jesus speaks to them, their fear gives way to worship. How might his words "I am" contribute to this change in reaction?

MATTHEW 15

Jesus finds the causes of defilement inside a person rather than outside. He talks specifically about the human heart, the hidden center of the person where choices and decisions are made. Ask God to heal and transform your heart so that what comes forth from it will be pure and undefiled.

Think about the story of the Canaanite woman as an example of prayer. Why does Jesus respond favorably to her pleas? What about the woman's interaction with Jesus strikes you as praiseworthy?

MATTHEW 16

Linger over Jesus' response to Peter's confession of faith. Have you ever noticed that Jesus calls the community of disciples "my Church" rather than Peter's? Jesus is the one who builds the Church; he is the one who ensures that it withstands the assaults of hell. Thank him for this tremendous gift. Thank him for giving us a place where the truth of the gospel is preserved in spite of the waves of error and doubt washing over our world.

Jesus rebukes Peter for not thinking the things of God. One such thing is the role that suffering plays in the plan of God. By human calculations, suffering is at best meaningless and at worst a cruel evil that robs us of happiness. But what do divine calculations tell us about suffering?

MATTHEW 17

Jesus allows his divinity to shine through his humanity on the Mount of Transfiguration. What are Peter, James, and John supposed to learn from this unique experience? What does the vision of Jesus, coupled with the voice and cloud, reveal about the inner mystery of God?

A desperate father seeks the mercy of Jesus for his son. In the Gospel story, the boy is possessed by a demon that convulses him violently and endangers his life. Many of us have no direct experience of possession, but we all know the pain of watching people do things that hurt themselves. Perhaps you have a child or a friend that is caught up in evil and needs the intervention of Christ. Bring this person to Jesus in prayer and plead for his healing mercy.

MATTHEW 18

Jesus uses graphic language to speak about the grave danger of sin, especially the scandal of leading others into sin. Since he is not speaking literally about bodily dismemberment, what might the severed "hand" or the plucked out "eye" represent in our lives?

According to the Parable of the Unforgiving Servant, mercy is not only a gift to receive and cherish but a gift to be shared with others. It also highlights the glaring disproportion between the two. Withholding forgiveness of minor debts is inexcusable when we have been forgiven an unpayable mountain of debt. Take a moment to marvel at the enormity of God's mercy toward us.

MATTHEW 19

Jesus repeals Moses' permission to divorce and reaffirms the lifelong union of man and woman established at creation. If Moses allowed divorce owing to a hardness of heart among God's people, what does this imply about Jesus' work in the hearts of men and women? Ponder the richness of the grace of the Sacrament of Matrimony.

The image of a camel squeezing through the eye of a needle is unforgettable. It teaches us that people who are bloated with riches find it difficult to enter Christ's kingdom. Yet Jesus adds that "with God, all things are possible." How does having a divine perspective on wealth assist us in the Christian life?

MATTHEW 20

The Parable of the Workers in the Vineyard teaches that God is both just and generous. He never withholds what he promises, but sometimes he gives more than he promises. Recall some of the ways that God has blessed you beyond what you deserved and thank him.

Jesus defines greatness in terms of humble service and sacrifice for others. Allow this teaching to challenge you. Reflect on how Jesus lived by this standard of greatness, going all the way to the Cross for the benefit of others. He gained nothing by the deed; we gained everything by it. Ask God to increase your capacity for selfless service to others.

MATTHEW 21

Jesus insists that faith can make prayer amazingly effective. What keeps you from "moving mountains" by praying with strong faith? Ask the Lord to increase your faith and to make your desire for trustful prayer more fervent.

The Parable of the Two Children reminds us that life is determined by many choices. Perhaps you have fallen from your initial commitment to follow Christ and be a faithful member of his Church. Or perhaps you are just hearing the gospel for the first time. So long as your life continues, the option to "change your mind" and follow Christ remains.

MATTHEW 22

When Jesus responds to the question about taxes, he states that images belong to their makers. The coin for the tax is stamped with the image of Caesar, and so it should be given back to him. We, however, are stamped with the image of God, and so we should give ourselves back to God. Ponder what it means to be made in God's image and consider what responsibilities this implies.

According to Jesus, the Law of Moses and the writings of the prophets hang on two precepts: the commandment to love God, and the commandment to love our neighbor. The Old Testament, in other words, teaches God's people how to love. Keep this in mind as you reflect on the Scriptures. Loving God and neighbor is the overarching lesson of the Bible, not just in the New Testament but also in the Old.

MATTHEW 23

Hypocrisy is not a unique failing of the scribes and Pharisees. It is also a temptation for Christians. We profess to be followers of Christ, but we often fail to practice what we preach. The same is true of religious show, the wearing of our piety on our sleeves for all to see. Say a prayer that Christ will strengthen you against these temptations and give you the grace of humility and obedience.

MATTHEW 24

Jesus prophesied the destruction of the Jerusalem temple in his own generation and the passing away of heaven and earth in the future. The first prophecy was fulfilled in A.D. 70 during the Roman conquest of Jerusalem; the second awaits fulfillment at the end of history. Ask yourself why Jesus made these events known ahead of time. If Jesus prophesied the end, what should we do to prepare for it?

Jesus promises to come again as the glorified Son of Man. Far from dreading this future event, Christians through the centuries have longed for the Second Coming. Imagine the intense joy that will sweep over the Church when she sees Christ coming in all his majesty. Say a prayer for the destruction of evil and the final unveiling of God's kingdom.

MATTHEW 25

The Parable of the Talents is about stewardship. Not everyone has been given the same gifts, but each has been given some gift. God expects us to invest our "talents" for his glory, and so failure to use God's gifts is not an option for a good and faithful servant. Reflect for a moment on the talents that God has given you. Commit yourself to investing them for the good of the Church and the world.

Think about the vision of the Last Judgment. Marvel at the authority that Christ the King wields over all people and nations of the world. Tremble in holy fear before this final separation of the sheep and the goats. Notice too how the works of mercy are anything but optional. Our salvation depends in part on serving Christ in the needy.

MATTHEW 26

At the Last Supper, Jesus says that his blood is "poured out" in the cup "for the forgiveness of sins." This implies a relationship between the Eucharist and the Cross as well as a relationship between the Eucharist and our salvation. Reflect on this for a moment and thank God for the mercy that flows into your life from the Lord's Table.

Notice how the mystery of Jesus' humanity and divinity is set before us in this chapter. In the Garden of Gethsemane, his humanity dreads the tortures and insults that await him. Yet, as he stands before the high priest, he accepts the charge of being "the Son of God" who is destined to sit at the Father's right hand in heaven. Bow your soul in silence before this cardinal mystery of the Christian faith.

MATTHEW 27

Reflect on the mockery of Jesus and consider the irony of the situation. The soldiers poke fun at him by dressing him like a king and pretending to show him homage. They have no idea that this bloodied and humiliated man is the Lord of all creation. They are unaware of the truth of their own declaration of his kingship. Speak to Christ in your heart and thank him for enduring such scornful indignities to release sinners from the madness of mocking God.

Contemplate the fact that Jesus dies in prayer. Even during his final moments, when his body is racked with pain and is barely clinging to life, the words of the Psalms are upon his lips. He shows by example what death should be—a sacred time of communion with God. Ask the Lord for the grace of final perseverance and the grace of a holy and prayerful death.

MATTHEW 28

When the women at the tomb encounter the risen Christ, they touch him and worship him. Consider that this privilege of Easter morning is our privilege at very Mass. We too can touch the risen Body and Blood of the Lord, and we too can adore his Real Presence in our midst. Reflect on Holy Communion as our own encounter with the resurrected Jesus.

The final words of Jesus in the Gospel are a missionary mandate for the Church. She is tasked with evangelizing, catechizing, and sacramentalizing all nations on earth. Consider your own role in this Great Commission. Say a prayer that God will help you and your fellow Christians be effective witnesses of the gospel. Pray too for the success of the Church's missionaries throughout the world.